$ GREEN POWER $

Hippe Power

BLACK POWER

AMERICAN POWER

Jewish Power

FLOWER POWER

YOUTH POWER

LOVe PoWer

ELECTRIC POWER

FAT PoWer

FOOT POWER

BUTTON POWER

Christen Carter & Ted Hake

PRINCETON ARCHITECTURAL PRESS   NEW YORK

I COLLECT BUTTONS

angry button

BAN BUTTONS

DON'T READ THIS BUTTON

DO YOU HAVE ALL YOUR BUTTONS ?

this button is just an attempt to communicate.

IGNORE THIS BUTTON

UNBUTTON

WEARING BUTTONS is not enough

BUTTON POWER

BAN ... BUTTONS

MY BUTTON LOVES YOUR BUTTON

Introduction

Punch line. Political statement. Conversation piece. Souvenir. From the campaign trail to the rock tour, the pin-back button occupies a fascinating, wide-reaching, and largely undocumented place in American popular history. Buttons embody a people's history of American culture and politics, and this book—the first of its kind—collects the best of them, selected for their design and historical significance. ● Social media is today's most popular platform for self-expression, but the button preceded it as a way to tell others what was on your mind and as a tool to help spread an idea. No other form of wearable expression has yet to replace the humble button—and unlike social media, a button is something that you can literally stand behind. ● You'll see in these pages buttons for political campaigns (from presidential races to student council contests), for commercial products (overalls, seed spreaders, beer, personal computers), and for grassroots causes (environmental justice, civil rights, anti-war efforts). You'll also see buttons uniquely representative of their time, celebrating everything from Rube Goldberg's early cartoons to women's suffrage and from FDR's US Senate campaign to the Teenage Mutant Ninja Turtles. ● Organized into broad categories, the selected buttons range from 1896—the year buttons were invented—to 2020. That's 125 years of buttons! But wearable insignia have been around much longer than that—arguably since ancient Egypt. At the end of the nineteenth century, pin-back badges became cheap to manufacture thanks to advances in commercial printing and metal stamping. It became possible at that time to produce celluloid, used to protect the paper on which the design was printed, in thin, transparent sheets. Buttons immediately became an inexpensive and novel form of advertising. ● The earliest major use of pin-back buttons was in the world of politics, as a convenient way to declare support for a chosen candidate. The New Jersey firm Whitehead & Hoag, established makers of decorative ribbons and ribbon badges, invented the first pin-back button in 1896. The presidential campaigns of William McKinley and

his opponent, William Jennings Bryan, quickly embraced the button, with over two thousand unique designs produced between the June and July nominating conventions and Election Day in November. ● Buttons also caught on fast with product advertisers. At that time, people had little exposure to printed imagery, and it was a novelty to own a printed item. That same year, the makers of the High Admiral (Yellow Kid) cigarette declared that pin-back buttons were "the greatest fad of all." ●
In these pages, we trace defining moments and movements in US history, both large and small, and show how these events were graphically represented, argued over, and celebrated through buttons. You'll see our favorite buttons from our personal collections, like Ted's 1908 button from Long Beach, California, featuring a mermaid celebrating the city's Festival of the Sea (with lettering formed by little sea snakes), and Christen's very first punk button, a classic 1-inch button for the band X. We've also included examples from the advanced collections of a few of our friends to show you what, in our opinion, are the best and the most interesting button designs ever produced. ● This highly edited sample from the hundreds of thousands of button designs produced over the past 125 years is a primer on American popular culture and zeitgeist as well as a visual feast. While you may learn some valuable history, we hope that you'll see yourself reflected in these small, round images that spark memories and connections along the arcs of our lives.

Christen Carter *Chicago, Illinois*
Ted Hake *York, Pennsylvania*
2020

Advertising

From the very beginning, the pin-back button was recognized as an effective method of advertising. In 1896, visual images were not nearly as prevalent as they are today, and owning printed matter was a true novelty. With all the new products in development at the turn of the twentieth century, there was never a shortage of companies seeking to advertise their wares. ● Since buttons are meant to be worn, their designs often reveal the trends of their era. Beautiful and detailed designs showcased manure spreaders, handheld calculators, clothing, soap—you name it. The value of word-of-mouth advertising has always been key for brands; these tiny works of art were a way for companies to reach buyers, but buttons became cultural touchstones as well, allowing people to feel like a part of larger movements and to celebrate creativity and innovation. ● Upon introduction, buttons featured detailed illustrations, using multiple colors in crisp letterpress; very quickly, photographs and color became popular, as four-color process printing became the standard for commercial printing.

DRINK **Mountain Dew**
1950

12 11 10 9 8 7 6 5 4 3 2 1
TIME TO DRINK
WHITE HOUSE
COFFEE
1912

MADE WITH
Sun Spot
REAL ORANGE JUICE
Sun Spot
1953

Quality MILK
NONE BETTER
Q
QUALITY DAIRY CO.
ST. LOUIS
1936

EXCLUSIVE WITH
HI-HAT
ICE CREAM SODA
10¢
McCRORY'S
1938

STANDARD BREWING CO.
ALE
CAN'T BE BEAT
ROCHESTER, N.Y.
1906

Coca-Cola
1919

MAGNOLIA COFFEE
1925

THE UNCOLA
7up
1967

Lemmy
LEMONADE
1939

DON'T MONKEY WITH ANY OTHER KIND
MONKEY COFFEE
1900

SATANET
the DRINK WITH A WINK
1914

Dottie Dimple: first button to use a literary character to endorse a product

1897

The use of fictional characters to endorse consumer products began in the mid-1880s, when the Brownies of Canadian-born artist Palmer Cox went to work plugging goods such as Estey pianos, Chocolate Cream Drops candy, Bee soap, Snag-Proof rubber boots, and Luden's cough drops. Character licensing has since grown into a multibillion-dollar industry. The first character to appear on a button was Dottie Dimple, featured on a 1¼-inch button from the Buffalo, New York, firm of O. P. Ramsdell Sweet & Co. The character was the creation of Rebecca Sophia "Sophie May" Clarke, whose forty-five books published between 1860 and 1903 earned her the title "the Dickens of the nursery." Her nieces were the inspiration for her book characters Little Prudy, Susy, and Dotty Dimple. It is unlikely that Clarke received any licensing fee, because her character was named Dotty Dimple while the shoe brand was spelled Dottie.

The teddy bear: inspired by President Theodore Roosevelt

ca. 1903

This 1¼-inch specimen is the earliest known advertising button to depict a teddy bear; it was issued by the Big Store in Milford, New Hampshire. The rather incongruous origin of this stuffed animal dates to late 1902, when Mississippi Governor Andrew Longino invited President Roosevelt on a bear hunting trip. When Roosevelt had not killed a bear after three days, the hunting guides proceeded to track and wound an old black bear, which they tied to a tree. Roosevelt refused to violate the spirit of sportsmanship by shooting the suffering animal, although he instructed that the bear be killed to end its misery. Newspaper coverage of the event inspired cartoonist Clifford Berryman to draw a cartoon of TR refusing to shoot the bear, which ran in the *Washington Post* on November 26, 1902. In Brooklyn, candy shop owner Morris Michtom and his wife, Rose, saw the cartoon and made two stuffed bear toys. They sent one to Roosevelt, asking permission to call them "Teddy's bears." Permission granted, Michtom ramped up production in 1903. The bears proved immensely popular and eventually became the basis for the Ideal Novelty and Toy Company.

1911

1898

1909

1938

I AM A KUTE KIX KID
NOYES-NORMAN SHOE CO.
I WEAR KUTE KIX
1923

WORTH HATS
HARRIS-POLK HAT CO.
1925

CANNED FOODS WEEK
If it's in a Can it's fresh!
NOVEMBER 8 to 15
1924

THE PREMIER CLEANER
FIRST AMONG CLEANERS
1921

Hohner Harmonicas bring Health with Happiness
1934

5¢ 10¢
1926

NOT-A-TOY
DEVELOPS THE BABY
CANNOT UPSET CANNOT FALL OUT
USED IN RESEARCH AND WELFARE WORK BY BABY WELFARE ASS'N, PHILA. PA.
1921

YOUR PLUMBER IS YOUR FRIEND
HE RECOMMENDS COP-R-LOY PIPE
1936

Clean-up Week
Chases Dirt
The Symbol of Healthful Cleanliness
1936

FASTEST ON EARTH
POSTAL TELEGRAPH
1935

FEELING FINE
JUST HAD MY CHERRY CLUSTER
1929

TRADE MARK
STEIFF TOY ANIMALS
LOOK FOR BUTTON IN EAR
1934

LOS PRODUCTOS IDEALES DESEADOS POR LA DAMA ELEGANTE
Pashon
PRODUCTOS DE BELLEZA
1937

SUNDAY WORLD S.F.C.
1925

Kills Germs
SPALDING'S PILLOW SANITIZING PROCESS
60¢ each
Fluffs Feathers
1934

BABY BEAR BREAD
1937

Let Van-Sal do Your Worrying
THERE'LL ALWAYS BE VANILLA
THE WORRIER
S.H. MAHONEY EXTRACT CO. CHICAGO
1937

"AN APPLE A DAY IS DOC APPLE'S WAY"
Doc Apple
Quality Brands of Apples
Reg. U.S. Pat. Off.
1936

LUCKY TIGER
CURES DANDRUFF
1935

THE DELIVERY SYSTEM
FOR STORES OF QUALITY
UPS
SINCE 1907
OUTING 1940

1940

BETTER THAN EVER
Frigidaire
for
'41
INSIDE AND OUT

1941

RCA VICTOR
19 39
MAGIC BRAIN "Q" MODELS

1939

Odorless
DRY
CLEANING

SANFORD BOX CLEANING SYSTEM

1936

GIMBEL'S

1938

THE NEW FASHION
Revlon
"AMERICAN WAY" MANICURE

1937

MAKE WAY FOR
MAYTAG IN '39

1939

SEARS
GOLDEN
JUBILEE
1886 1936

1936

SHOPPING DAY'S
UNTIL 1 2 3
4 5 6 7 8 9 10
11 12 13 14 15 16 17
18 19 20 21 22 23 24
25 CHRISTMAS

Muntz TV
Vernon 1200

1947

Follow thru
IN 40
WITH
Hotpoint

1940

FISH
PECKERWOOD CLUB
CHICKEN
FROG LEGS
Mittieville
LEXINGTON Mo
BEER
LAMB FRYS

1948

"THE ALPS"
NEW YORK
WORLD'S BEST FOOD

1938

Hello
MY NAME IS
JOE STONE
RECOMMENDING
KOERBER'S
PILSENER
TO YOU

1939

THE TINY TWINS
IM GAS   IM ELECTRICITY
G E
OF THE
BUDGET FAMILY

1939

HORSES NEIGH FOR **5A** Blankets

1907

FROG IN YOUR THROAT? 10¢ FOR COUGHS AND COLDS

TRADE MARK

1901

WURLITZER-CINCINNATI

VICTOR

"HIS MASTER'S VOICE"

1902

CHOLERINE FOR FOWLS

1918

"Professor" Mac Levy: physical fitness entrepreneur, Brooklyn

ca. 1904

Mac (born Max) Levy grew up as the prover-
bial ninety-eight-pound weakling, but by
the turn of the twentieth century, he had
transformed himself through diet and
exercise into the vaudeville and lecture attraction
known as the "Young Hercules," or "Brooklyn's Perfect
Man." Levy established a gymnasium and health club
at the upscale Hotel St. George in Brooklyn Heights,
operated summer health clubs, taught the proper use
of dumbbells, invented a famous rowing machine for
exercise, and still had time to offer "Swimming Taught
in Six Lessons," promoted on this gorgeous 1¾-inch
button produced by the Baltimore Badge & Novelty
Company. There are just two known examples remaining of this rare button featuring nine lovely female
heads floating above blue ocean water.

Arby's **ROAST BEEF** Sandwich IS DELICIOUS

ADVERTISED IN **LIFE**

1965

U.S. MAIL

MR. ZIP

1963

MALTEX AND **MAYPO** HEALTH CLUB

1956

HEY CULLIGAN® MAN!

1961

Business is **GOOD**

Find It Fast In The 'Yellow Pages'

1963

A CRAZY

101

MILLIMETER LONGER

1967

King Congo

Carpets by **Congoleum**

1968

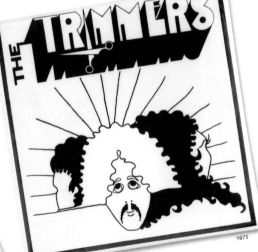

THE TRIMMERS

1973

BENIHANA For the fun of it.

1977

C

® CAP'N CRUNCH

1965

Twoallbe efpattiesspe cialsaucelettuc echeesepickles onionsonasesa meseedbun.

McDonald's

1974

THE MENEHUNES ARE COMING TO TRADER VIC'S

1970

YES!

THANKS NICE KID!

LET THE RABBIT EAT TRIX!

1976

You only lick once

e-z wider

1982

NO!

AW SHUCKS

TRIX ARE FOR KIDS!

1976

RIZLA

ROLLS THE WORLD!

1979

ann taylor 25th Anniversary

1978

the gap

1974

Try our cool new dessert

JELL-O® BRAND

Pudding Pops™

Frozen pudding on a stick

chocolate • vanilla • banana

1980

2007

swatch SWISS

1986

I CAN HANDLE THE MONSTER

SUPER GIANT

1978

Lisa Frank inc.

1980

Where's the Beer?

1984

KICK STARTER .COM

2010

Comfort Soap: the first product-endorsement button by the "What, Me Worry?" kid

ca. 1905

The mascot of *MAD* magazine made his debut in November 1954 on the front cover of a paperback book of reprints from the humor magazine's first two years. Two years later, artist Norman Mingo painted the defining portrait and editor Al Feldstein named the "What, Me Worry?" boy Alfred E. Neuman. His image, original artist unknown, traces back to an ad for an 1894 Broadway comic play titled *The New Boy* and an 1895 advertisement for Atmore's Mince Meat. This 1¾-inch Comfort Soap example is his first product endorsement button. He also appears on a 1900 military veterans' button (see page 174); a 1940 anti–Franklin D. Roosevelt / pro–Wendell Willkie campaign button (see page 61); and a 1941 button for the Superior company, makers of gambling punch-boards (see page 29).

1988

1987

1987

1981

1985

1987

1983

1981

High Performance
IBM Personal Computers

1984

1985

1989

Arts & Entertainment

Buttons have served the entertainment industry for more than a century, documenting the history of popular culture: cartoons, film, TV, music, performances, amusement rides, and literature appear on some of the most beloved examples. Buttons featuring every generation's heroes and touchstones—icons such as the Yellow Kid of 1896 (see page 26), Rin Tin Tin in the 1930s (see page 28), and Keith Haring in the 1980s (see page 49)—define us and help us to recall large portions of our lives. ● Pop culture reflects the time in which it was created and the cultural values that we have idealized. Buttons promoting vaudeville actors and silent movie stars created an intimacy with their fans. Through them, people could gaze at their favorite stars any time. From the 1950s on, buttons brought musical heartthrobs like Elvis, the Beatles, and BTS into the hands of generations of teenagers worldwide.

WONDER WOMAN READING CLUB
INGLEWOOD PUBLIC LIBRARY
TM and © 1981 DC COMICS INC
1981

R.R.·S JONES CADETS
US
1941

· READ SUPERMAN DAILY · IN THE DEMOCRAT ·
STRENGTH · COURAGE · JUSTICE
1939

CAPTAIN MARVEL CLUB
SHAZAM
1972

WONDER WOMAN
SENSATION COMICS
1942

SUPERMAN
1945

MEMBER
DICK TRACY
SECRET SERVICE PATROL
1938

KEEP IT UP, AMERICA.
KEEP SAVING ENERGY.
© 1980 MCG
1980

THE GREEN HORNET
1966

CAPTAIN MARVEL CLUB
SHAZAM
1946

THE GREEN HORNET ADVENTURE CLUB
A NEW UNIVERSAL PICTURE
1940

Ideal
MIGHTY MOUSE
© TERRYTOONS · MADE IN U.S.A. By IDEAL NOVELTY & TOY CO. HOLLIS 7, N.Y.
1952

Beautiful Jim Key: equine rights advocate

ca. 1904 This famous turn-of-the-twentieth-century performing horse "was taught by kindness" and never a whip by "Dr." William Key, a former slave, self-taught veterinarian, and patent medicine salesman. Traveling in a special railcar, Dr. Key and Jim appeared in the best venues in large cities to amaze the crowds and champion the fledgling concept of the humane treatment of animals. After appearing at Madison Square Garden, Jim began a long stint at the 1904 St. Louis World's Fair, where he was among the most popular attractions. Along the way, "I Have Seen Beautiful Jim Key" 1¼-inch buttons became cherished souvenirs. Jim could spell words by grasping letter plaques in his teeth and placing them in correct order, do arithmetic "for numbers below thirty," and operate a cash register. It is claimed that through the twenty-seven thousand North American Band of Mercy humane-education clubs, Jim got two million kids to pledge never to be mean to animals. George Angell's American Humane Education Society made Beautiful Jim Key an honorary member.

"FOXY GRANDPA"
JOSEPH HART AND CARRIE DeMAR
BUNNY
1902

HERSHEY PARK
1906

NEW YORK HERALD
YOUNG FOLKS.
1902

JAMES T POWERS
IN THE BLUE MOON
1906

PHILADELPHIA PRESS
BILLY BOUNCE
1905

LET'S GO TO LUNA PARK
1903

Lithography is an Art
1912

HAVE YOU SEEN THE SHOW SAY AT THE FOSS
1907

Paramount Pictures
1917

MILLIE DeLEON
The Girl In Blue
QUEEN OF ALL DANCERS
1906

MIDNIGHT AT MAXIM'S
1915

THE GREAT COAL MINE
CONEY ISLAND
1907

ANNIE REDLINE
WT. 568
1909

Read the new Baum Book The Scarecrow of OZ
1915

HIHESHA THE GIRL WITH POETIC LEGS
1920

AROUND THE WORLD
JACK AND JANET
1915

WELCOME CLARA BOW
1927

LITTLE HIP AND HIS PROF. ANDRE OWNER
1915

DOUGLAS FAIRBANKS The BLACK PIRATE
STRAND THEATRE
1926

TOM MIX FOR SHERIFF
1920

CHICAGO HERALD COMIC PICTURE CLUB
1915

ORPHAN ANNIE
HAROLD GRAY
1931

"FREAKS"
METRO-GOLDWYN-MAYER'S AMAZING PICTURE
1932

WE MOURN OUR LOSS
RUDOLPH VALENTINO
1926

COUNT PEPITO JOSEPHINE BAKER IN THE SIREN OF THE TROPICS COMING TO YOUR FAVORITE THEATRE
1927

LAUREL AND HARDY
1932

THEY AFRAID OF THE BIG BAD WOLF
1933

DONALD DUCK "WANNA FIGHT"
© WALT DISNEY ENTERPRISES
1935

Meet FELIX at PLAZA Theatre
1932

LEBANON CO. FIREMEN'S CONVENTION
JUNE 20-1931
FD
1931

LOONEY TUNE CLUB
1932

© KFS 1936
JEEP
1936

BUTTERFLY PICTURES
1920

"Smookums"
in the NEWLYWEDS AND THEIR BABY
A STERN BROS. COMEDY
1928

RIN-TIN-TIN FAN CLUB
A WARNER BROS. STAR
1931

LOEW'S OUR GANG CLUB
4783
1929

AMERICAN FEDERATION OF ACTORS
CIRCUS DIVISION
AFA
AFFILIATED WITH
AMERICAN FEDERATION OF LABOR
C-1907
1938

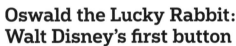

"OSWALD"
THE LUCKY RABBIT

Oswald the Lucky Rabbit: Walt Disney's first button

1927

Walt Disney (1901–1966) and his brother, Roy (1893–1971), founded the Disney Brothers Cartoon Studio on October 16, 1923. Their focus by early 1927 was an energetic rabbit named Oswald, created by their studio with the financial backing of film producer Charles Mintz. By August 1928, twenty-six cartoons had been finished and distributed by Universal Studios. Quality improved with each release but at an expense requiring a budget increase. Walt went to New York seeking additional funding but got a shock when Mintz instead demanded a 20 percent cut in the cost of each cartoon. Mintz pointed out that contractually, Universal owned the character and that if Walt didn't like the terms, Mintz could produce the Oswald series without him. Walt made the painful decision to part ways with Oswald. On the train home to California, he did a few simple drawings of a mouse named Mortimer. Later renamed Mickey (because Walt's wife, Lillian, disliked the sound of "Mortimer Mouse") and refined by animator Ub Iwerks, Mickey Mouse and his girlfriend, Minnie, were unveiled to the public on November 18, 1928, at the Colony Theater in New York. *Steamboat Willie* was the world's first sound cartoon and the start of Disney's empire.

FOLLOW THE ADVENTURES OF
FLASH GORDON
BUSTER CRABBE
MOVIE CLUB
1938

· THE WORLD'S DARLING ·
GENUINE SHIRLEY TEMPLE DOLL
1935

LI'L ABNER
1935

BUCK ROGERS in the 25th CENTURY
1935

ELLA CINDERS
NOW IN THE
EXAMINER
1937

ED WYNN IN The CHIEF
A METRO Goldwyn Mayer PICTURE
1933

A NIGHT AT THE MOULIN ROUGE
HELEN MORGAN
1939

PREMIERE "GONE WITH THE WIND"
ATLANTA, GA.
1939

betty boop
© FLEISCHER STUDIOS
1930

GRETA GARBO
1935

CHARLIE CHAPLIN in
"MODERN TIMES"
LOEW'S STARTS FRIDAY
1936

The "LONE RANGER"
COMIC
DAILY and SUNDAY
EXAMINER
1938

WORLDS
CLARKE GABLE and VIVIEN LEIGH
GONE WITH THE WIND
ATLANTA
1939
PREMIERE

ALL IN FAVOR OF SWING SAY AYE
SAYS TOMMY DORSEY
1939

FRANK CAPRA'S "MR. SMITH GOES TO WASHINGTON."
I'M A SMITH
HE'S A JOLLY GOOD FELLOW!
1939

Mickey ROONEY - Judy GARLAND
"BABES IN ARMS"
BOYD
19th CHESTNUT
1939

JUDY GARLAND
DOLL
1940

WHY GIRLS LEAVE HOME
1945

THE PHANTOM CREEPS Adventure Club
A New UNIVERSAL Picture
1939

ME WORRY?
SUPERIOR - 1941
1941

554
WIZARD OF OZ
JUDY GARLAND
M-G-M's
1939

THE MILTON BERLE
MAKE-UP CLUB
1946

MY HERO
FRANK SINATRA
1942

Fun Club: member's button from the first comic book–sponsored club

1935

Major Malcolm Wheeler-Nicholson (1890–1965), a cavalry officer and former pulp magazine writer, struck upon the idea of a comic book containing only original (as opposed to reprinted) material in late 1934. Titled *New Fun*, the first issue hit newsstands with a cover dated February 1935. Printed as a 10-by-15-inch tabloid, it had color covers and black-and-white interior pages of stories, humor, and games. The early issues recruited club members, who were awarded this button and a membership certificate. With issue number 7, the title became *More Fun*. Not only was the publication among the first to publish original material, but it was also the first to publish work by Walt Kelly (later of *Pogo* fame) and Jerome Siegel and Joseph Shuster, who achieved fame a few years later as Superman's creators. *New Fun* became the cornerstone of the DC Comics publishing empire.

CANADA DRY
Mary Hartline
SUPER CIRCUS CLUB
1950

MEMBER DOC & LOOKIE SAFETY CLUB
DIAL 1150 WCUE
1949

HOWDY DOODY FOR PRESIDENT
1952

PETE PIRATE
GOOD LUCK KGNC-TV
1959

KARL THE KARROT
KEDS KLUB
1955

ANNIE OAKLEY
QUINCY MAID
1954

DYNAMO DUDLEY
ROBOT POLICE
1955

I'VE TALKED TO FRANCIS
STERLING · LINDNER · DAVIS' TALKING MULE
1949

WQED
1960

WOODY WOODPECKER
HI PAL!
1957

1955

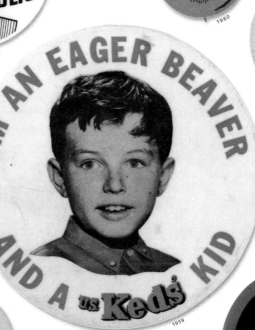

I'M AN EAGER BEAVER AND A US Keds KID
1959

RIN TIN TIN
1959

and away-a-gy we go!!!!
Jackie Gleason fan club
1957

YABADABADOO
FRED FLINTSTONE
1961

BARNEY
1961

"BUGS BUNNY"
WHAT'S UP DOC?
1959

I'LL SAY THESE ARE GREAT CAPS *Wesley Barry*

1920

RENO BROWNE · QUEEN OF THE WESTERNS

1949

DICK TRACY JUNIOR

1933

MEMBER UNCLE·WIGGILY·CLUB

1925

THE LONE RANGER

1956

BORRAH MINEVITCH JUNIOR HARMONICA RASCAL CLUB

1937

JUNIOR OLYMPIC CLUB *Sonja Henie*

1936

Rootie Kazootie Club ROOTIE KAZOOTIE

1952

GEORGE "GABBY" HAYES

1951

MY NAME IS JAZZ HERALD AND EXAMINER ©1923 F.W.H.

1923

DAVY CROCKETT

1955

ZORRO

1957

Roney's Boys: the first band buttons

ca.
1901 &
1903

"I'm Going to Hear Roney's Boys / Are You?" was a phrase uttered from Missoula, Montana, to Buffalo, New York. It referred to a Chicago-based traveling group of five boy musicians under the direction of Henry B. Roney, trainer, originator, and manager. As a way to help wayward boys, he taught his constantly rotating cast to sing hymns (until their voices started to change). Between 1888 and 1913, the Roney Boys Concert Co. provided "some of the sweetest music on this earth" for birthday parties, Sunday school groups, and prison inmates. In 1903, they even performed a Christmas concert for five hundred children in the White House East Room at the invitation of First Lady Edith Roosevelt. Afterward, all enjoyed ice cream frozen into the shape of Santa Claus. In the first two buttons to picture a band, the Boys appear in either Scottish garb or patriotic red, white, and blue outfits.

Reuben Garrett Lucius Goldberg: I'm the guy…

ca. 1912 The parents of Rube Goldberg (1883–1970) didn't like the idea of a cartooning career and made him acquire an engineering degree. In 1904, straight out of school, he worked a few months for the San Francisco Water and Sewer Department, focusing on pipes. By 1905, he was trying his hand at sports cartoons, and by 1907, he was in New York City cartooning for the *New York Evening Mail*. By 1915, his cartoons were syndicated nationally and his name was known coast-to-coast. Today, he is best known for his cartoons showing complicated contraptions concocted to perform very simple tasks. By 1912 (and maybe earlier), Rube was drawing a four-panel cartoon titled *I'm the Guy*. The last panel always concluded with wordplay such as "I'm the guy that put the imp in shrimp." This gimmick became popular across America. In 1912, Rube published sheet music for his hit song "I'm the Guy," and the cigarette brands Hassan and Tokio packaged with their products millions of ⅞-inch buttons that all began: "I'm the guy that put the…" Each of these buttons pictures one of seventeen Goldberg-drawn cartoon men combined with one of fifty-seven known slogans such as "…con in Congress," in eye-catching color combinations. Other cartoonists of the era (including Bud Fisher of *Mutt and Jeff*) produced a few "I'm the guy…" buttons for Hassan and Tokio, bringing the total of known "I'm the guy…" full-color buttons to seventy-nine.

JEFF'S COLLIE CLUB

1959

SEE *Barbarella* DO HER THING!

1968

THE ADDAMS FAMILY

1964

"FLIPPER"

1964

SIMON THEODORE ALVIN

1962

HEY! LET'S TWIST

1961

VOTE FOR ZACHERLY

1963

Maratona: snake handler

ca. 1910

Maratona existed: the evidence is her oversize 2½-inch photographic button. This perfectly poised circus celebrity stares confidently into the camera, oblivious to the giant snake draped over her head and shoulders. This seems to be the sole surviving button to picture her. No further information about Maratona has come to light; the authors welcome any such information.

MARATONA

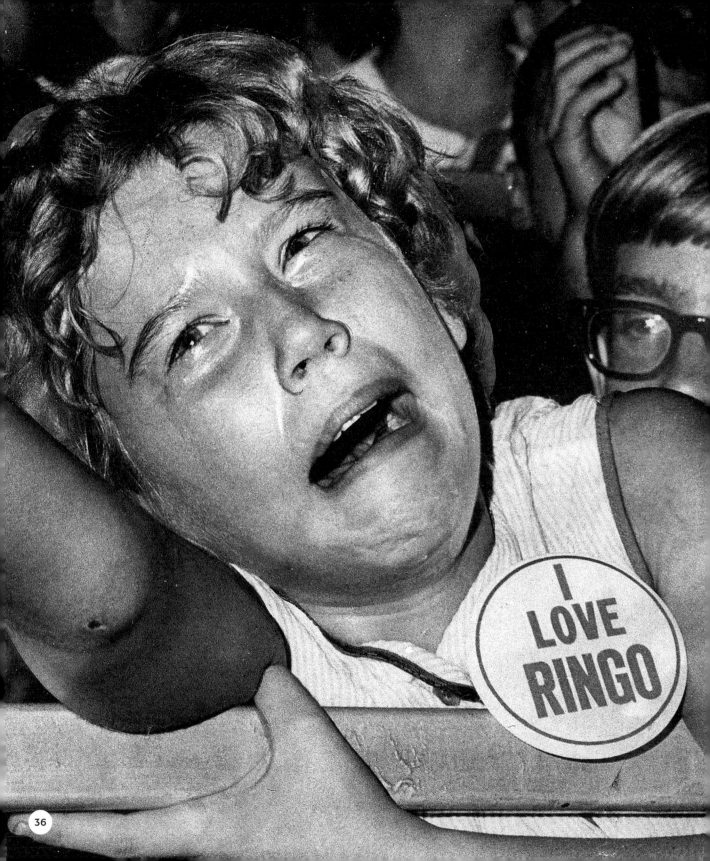

I AM A PURPLE PEOPLE EATER

1958

GO, MAN, GO! CRAZY, MAN, CRAZY!

1955

HELP STAMP OUT THE BEATLES

1964

BO DIDDLEY · THE DUCHESS & JEROME FAN CLUB

1958

ROCK 'N' ROLLETTES

1957

I LIKE ELVIS

1956

PAT BOONE 4TH ANNIVERSARY

1959

I HATE ELVIS

1956

Dr. Jive: rhythm and blues becomes rock and roll

1955

Tommy "Dr. Jive" Smalls was a rhythm and blues DJ from 1947 to 1960. The first African American radio DJ in Savannah, Georgia, he moved to New York in 1952 and DJed for WWRL, where he became immensely popular, selling out venues all over New York and often at the Apollo Theater. In November 1955, he had the opportunity to introduce some musical acts on the Ed Sullivan Show, bringing the sounds of Harlem to mainstream America through performances by Bo Diddley, LaVern Baker, Willis "Gator Tail" Jackson, and the Five Keys. His DJ career ended when he was caught accepting money to play certain records in a payola scandal involving other DJs, including Alan Freed and Dick Clark. On this button, Smalls advertises Birdel's, a record shop that was a mainstay of Brooklyn's Bedford-Stuyvesant neighborhood.

DR. JIVE BIRDEL'S FOR RECORDS

"LIMELIGHT ON LIZA"

LIZA MINNELLI

1964

TOODY
For PRESIDENT

1962

MULDOON
For PRESIDENT

1962

Q

I'M FOR THE MANCHURIAN CANDIDATE

1962

TINY TIM
President & First Lady

1968

eye

1968

PAT PAULSEN
FOR PRESIDENT

1968

'woodstock'
peace and music

1970

BULLWINKLE FOR PRESIDENT
IN YOUR HEART IT'S A LOT OF BULL

1972

DINAH SHORE FAN CLUB

1974

HERE'S JOHNNY

1972

RON RILEY'S **BATMAN CLUB** WLS/WBKB-TV
1966

peter max
1968

BILL GRAHAM presents BLUES-ROCK BASH II BUTTERFIELD BLUES BAND JEFFERSON AIRPLANE MUDDY WATERS IN DANCE-CONCERT AT WINTERLAND FRIDAY AND SAT NIGHTS SEP 23, 24 • SEP 30, OCT 1 SUNDAY AFTERNOONS SEP 25 OCT 2 COLUMBUS AVE QUESTIONS CALL 567-4800
1966

IN THE NIGHT KITCHEN MAURICE SENDAK
1970

RICHARD PRYOR "CRAPS" ON LAFF
1971

PINBALL WIZARD
1973

THE EXORCIST comes JUNE 19
1974

HAIR
1968

CAFE WHA?

THE UNDERGROUND TONIGHT SHOW

1974

Pray for Rosemary's Baby

1968

IT'S NOT MY JOB!

CHICO AND THE MAN

NBC

1975

BIG, BLACK, BEAUTIFUL PROUD AND UGLY CLUB KATZ 1600

1975

NEW YORK CITY BALLET

1975

CAROL BURNETT

HOUSEKEEPING AWARD

1974

STARSKY & HUTCH

1976

JOFFREY '76

1976

MARTHA, MARGOT & RUDI

1975

STEVE McQUEEN is a doll.

1975

REALLY ROSIE

1975

2001

THE
ULTIMATE
TRIP

1968

© 1975 UNIVERSAL PICTURES & COFFER SPORTS OF NORTHAMPTON

JAWS

1975

E.T.™

1982

LABYRINTH

1986

1976

MARY HARTMAN FOR PRESIDENT

1976

the anchorpersons are here!

ABC NEWS

1976

AMERICAN REVOLUTION BICENTENNIAL 1776-1976

1976

GET DOWN AMERICA! VOTE HOWARD THE DUCK IN '76

1976

FONZIE for PRESIDENT

THE PINNING CO. 8556 Venice Blvd. L.A. CA 90034

©1976 Paramount Pictures Corp.

1976

1977

LINDA RONSTADT FOR 1st LADY

1980

STAR TREK

1978

Annie
A New Musical

1976

MARCH 29-30, 1980

MC 5 - DEAD BOYS
KNOW - TROGGS

I SURVIVED THE ROCKAGES WAITING LINE

1980

GOD SAVE THE QUEEN

1977

THE ROCKY HORROR PICTURE SHOW

1978

Mork from Ork™

1979

JOHNNY · JOEY · DEE DEE · TOMMY

1978

LUNAR POWER!

Llewellyn's
Moon Sign
Book

1979

ELTON JOHN

CENTRAL PARK—1980
KEEP IT GREEN

1980

DOCTOR WHO

©1980 BBC ENTERPRISES

1980

J.R. EWING FOR PRESIDENT

1980

1980

1978

1966

1982

1981

ONCE A TWIT ALWAYS A TWIT

1980

MTV MUSIC TELEVISION™

1982

GRAFF

1982

BEE GEES

The Tape of the Stars

AMPEX

1981

CATS

NEW YORK OCTOBER 7, 1982

1982

EXPRESSION of the DANCE

1981

KRAFTWERK

1981

1983

I ♥ Michael Jackson

1983

THE DUKES OF HAZZARD™

01

TM Indicates Trademark of Warner Bros., Inc.

1983

Vampire Lesbians of Sodom

1984

ZZ TOP

ELIMINATOR

1983

Better Badges: buttons are punk

1976

When the Ramones played the Roundhouse in London on July 4, 1976, the British punk scene was deeply and forever influenced by American garage punk. It was also the moment punk buttons were born. Joly MacFie, a self-described hippie, made a batch of Ramones buttons and sold them at this show. He started his button-making company, Better Badges,* using the rallying cry of "Image as virus, disease as cure." MacFie sold directly to fans at a "pin stall" at the Roundhouse and also provided bands with custom-made buttons. Hundreds of bands big and small, including the Buzz-cocks and X-Ray Spex, used Better Badges services. His tenure at Better Badges from 1976 to 1982 marks the beginning and the end of the punk era in London; if it weren't for MacFie, buttons wouldn't be the punk fashion staple they were and still are today.

*Button : US :: badge : UK

RAMBO
FIRST BLOOD PART II

1984

WORK IS HELL

©1984 BY MATT GROENING

A NEW CARTOON BOOK BY MATT GROENING

1984

STRANGERS OF OTHER WORLD LISTENING IN ON TALKING HEADS

1985

The New Beat Generation©
Boy George

1984

IRVIN FELD and KENNETH FELD
PRESENT

Siegfried & Roy

Superstars of Magic

IN BEYOND BELIEF

FRONTIER
HOTEL & CASINO / LAS VEGAS

1983

Cabbage Patch Kids

1983

PUNKY BREWSTER

1985

NICKELODEON®

1985

ARTS & ENTERTAINMENT 47

BOOK IT!℠

1985

MADONNA

1987

1986

REFINED ANGRY WIRED

Penguin Books

RAW

1989

FREE

MARVEL SUPER-HEROES® CUPS

©1986 MCG

1986

GREMLINS

STRIPE is a Gremlin.

1984

WALL STREET

COMING THIS CHRISTMAS

1987

THE JONESES ARE COMING

HOLD ON TO YOUR HATS

1989

LEONARDO™

1988 MIRAGE STUDIOS

1988

MAX HEADROOM

1987

1986

1975

1980

1984

1973

1985

1984

1986

KRUSTY FOR PRESIDENT

OF ALL THE CLOWNS RUNNING, HE'S THE BEST

MATT GROENING

1992

THE SIMPSONS™

MATT GROENING

1989

ALVIN AILEY®
american dance theater

JUDITH JAMISON
ARTISTIC DIRECTOR

1989

KID 'N PLAY

LOCKER ROOM

CLASS ACT

PREMIERE

1992

1992

BRAM STOKER'S
Dracula

A FRANCIS FORD COPPOLA FILM

1992

OZ®

know
that
look.

Seinfeld™

1993

TIM BURTON'S
NIGHTMARE BEFORE
CHRISTMAS

1993

"THAT'S COOL"

MTV's BEAVIS AND BUTT-HEAD

1993

1993

GARGOYLES

1994

MIGHTY MORPHIN POWER RANGERS THE MOVIE

1995

CATHY™
QUEEN OF THE STRIPS

1993

the budget girls

1995

Frank Frazetta

only from Xerotik

1994

Gary Larson's
The Far Side
SCREEN SAVER COLLECTION

DELRINA

1994

OFFICIAL MEMBER
RADIOACTIVE MAN'S THERMONUCLEAR THRONG

1996

F·R·I·E·N·D·S

1995

AFRO PUNK

2012

2003

SMART
FEARLESS
HEROIC

XENA
WARRIOR PRINCESS

1997

2003

2010

BUGS & MICHAEL   A MAJOR MOVIE EVENT

1995

KingPiN

1996

BALDWIN ★ FEY
ALL THE WAY!

2008

gos
sip

2010

2013

I ♥
KAZAKH-
STAN

© 2007 FOX

2007

2011

나만추

2013

COMIC-CON® 2019

4 of 5   © PNTS

2019

2013

Campaigns & Causes

The celluloid-covered pin-back button introduced in 1896 was a direct descendant of metal clothing buttons made in 1789 to commemorate the presidential inauguration of George Washington. The next big advance in wearable communication devices came five decades later, with the wave of technology that accompanied the 1840 presidential contest between William Harrison and running mate John Tyler ("Tippecanoe and Tyler Too") versus Martin Van Buren and Richard Johnson. That contest saw an explosion of glass-covered brass badges (mostly picturing Harrison's mythical log cabin birthplace) that were affixed to garments with a reverse bar pin and clasp. In 1860, Abraham Lincoln and his opponents Stephen A. Douglas, John Bell, and John C. Breckinridge had their photographic images reproduced "from life," as was said, on hundreds of thousands of small iron- or tin-backed badges. During the 1870s, cardboard photos gradually replaced emulsion on metal. Celluloid, the material that made the modern pin-back button possible, was developed in 1856 and initially used as a replacement for ivory. The first wearable celluloid-covered novelties (lapel studs) were used in the 1888 presidential campaign between Benjamin Harrison and Grover Cleveland. Finally, on July 21, 1896, Whitehead & Hoag was granted the last in the series of patents that established the design of the pin-back button we know today. Ever since, buttons have been a perfect medium for the messages of campaigns and causes.

ALL YOU CAN GET From WILLKIE IS BUTTONS

1940

100 MILLION BUTTONS CAN'T BE WRONG

1940

Emancipation Proclamation Exposition, New York City

1913   This 1-inch button depicts Frederick Douglass (1818–1895). His life spanned slavery, escape, freedom, and national leadership of the abolitionist movement. This 1913 button honored him and marked the fiftieth anniversary of President Lincoln's executive order, effective January 1, 1863, that changed the federal legal status of over three-and-a-half-million enslaved African Americans. The idea of a celebration was widely discussed in 1909 (the centennial of Lincoln's birth), with Booker T. Washington and W. E. B. Du Bois urging President William Howard Taft and Congress to support a national commemoration. In Taft's first State of the Union address, he asked Congress for funds for a planning commission. No funds were forthcoming, but both Washington and Du Bois kept working. In the end, several states did hold celebrations; the most successful by far, with a ten-day run in late October 1913 and thirty thousand attendees, was New York City's event, spearheaded by Du Bois and organized by nine African American planning commission members.

FOR CONGRESS
WILLIAM RANDOLPH HEARST
1902

DO YOU SMOKE?
YES—SINCE 1896!
THAT'S WHAT McKINLEY PROMISED.
1900

GET IN THE BANDWAGON
1904

INTERNATIONAL CONVENTION
I.P.P. & A.U.
1900

FARMERS CONGRESS
"PIKES PEAK OR BUST"
AUG. 21 1900
COLORADO SPRINGS
1900

THE NATION IN SYMPATHY
1901

GIVE US LIBERTY
DOWN WITH THE CORRUPT POLITICAL MACHINE
1900

SEPT. 1 1902
LABOR·DAY
PORTLAND ORE.
1902

THE GOERKE CO.
WELCOME
1910

LABOR OMNIA VINCIT
Wm D. HAYWOOD — 1907
1907

FOR STATE SENATOR
FRANKLIN D. ROOSEVELT
1910

FOR U.S. SENATOR
FRANKLIN D. ROOSEVELT
1914

G.O.P.
1905

ROOSEVELT AND FAIRBANKS 1905

PARKER AND DAVIS
FAIRBANKS
JUDGE! WE'RE "IT"
1904

THIS BUTTON WILL SHOW THE PICTURE OF Democratic Candidate AS SOON AS NOMINATED
1904

EQUALITY
1904

THEIR ONLY CRIME
LOYALTY
TO THE WORKING CLASS
1906

Salvation Army Home Service Fund Campaign: "A Man May Be Down but He's Never Out"

1937 — This phrase appeared on a poster by Frederick Duncan for the Salvation Army Home Service Fund Campaign, held May 19–26, 1919—about a half year after the World War I armistice. It featured a young Salvation Army worker in her cape and bonnet as an uplifting force among a sea of destitute men, women, and children. On this ⅞-inch button, the image is a much simpler steaming-hot cup of coffee with three small doughnuts, still symbolizing hope for millions of downtrodden Americans during the Great Depression. This button is among millions issued during the Depression by local community groups raising funds for the general welfare.

Kick out
DEPRESSION
WITH A
DEMOCRATIC VOTE
1932

"LANDON ON THE NEW DEAL"
GOP
1936

Get your off the Grass It's DEWY
1948

I'LL BET MY
ON
WILLKIE
1940

MARCH 4 1913

THE REAL ISSUE
THE SALOON OR THE BOYS AND GIRLS
1911

SAN FRANCISCO LABOR MARTYRS
MOONEY BILLINGS
1916

ME FOR WHICH? THE BOY
1916

PROGRESSIVE
1912

CHAS. ALLEN SMITH
KILLED AT VERA CRUZ MEXICO
1914

I·A·OF M.
LABOR DAY 1910
1910

WILSON AND MARSHALL 1916
1916

POLITICAL AID SOCIETY OF MILWAUKEE
KARL MARX
RELIEF FOR POLITICAL EXILES IN SIBERIA
1917

OUR TONIC FOR MEXICO
1914

LENIN 1870-1924
MEMORIAL MEETING 1926
1926

DAVIS BRYAN
1924

HUGHES AND FAIRBANKS 1916
1916

COX AND ROOSEVELT
1920

My Country 'Tis of Thee
HOOVER AND CURTIS
100%
The CRISIS is HERE!
1928

I AM HELPING THE CHILDREN
BUY PLAYGROUND APPARATUS
Please let me play
1925

WASH. D.C.
COOLIDGE DAWES
MARCH 4, 1925
1925

NATIONAL WCTU
SAN FRANCISCO 1921
1921

"THEY SHALL NOT WANT"
WELFARE LEAGUE, LOUISVILLE 1921
1921

MASS PROTEST
WILL RELEASE THE FIGHTERS FOR THE UNEMPLOYED
INTERNATIONAL LABOR DEFENSE
1930

NRA CONSUMER U.S.
WE DO OUR PART
"ACE" BADGE, BUTTON & MEDAL CO. N.Y.C.
1933

HUEY P. LONG FOR PRESIDENT
1936

NO BEER NO WORK
1932

I GAVE 1927 MEMPHIS COMMUNITY CENTER FOR COLORED PEOPLE
1927

ALL AMERICA ANTI-IMPERIALIST LEAGUE
1925

SUPPORT WORK
DANCE LEAGUE
1933

1935

SAVE THE SCOTTSBORO BOYS
I.L.D.
1933

NO BEER - NO WORK
JULY 1ST
1932

REDUCE THE TAX
5¢ BEER
THE NICKLE BEER CLUB OF AMERICA
1936

BYE-BYE Mr. DRY YOU'RE ALL WET
1933

MILK FOR THE CHILDREN of LABOR PRISONERS
I.L.D.
1933

Franklin D. Roosevelt and James M. Cox: the most valuable pin-back button

1920

Any undamaged button from the 1920 presidential campaign picturing the Democratic nominees for president and vice president, Franklin D. Roosevelt and James M. Cox, has auction records in excess of ten thousand dollars. That includes the most common ⅞-inch brown-tone variety as well as the 1³⁄₁₆-inch "Americanize America" and the 1-inch "Cox Roosevelt Club," both of which have sold for around forty thousand dollars. The ever-elusive 1¼-inch variety doesn't have a modern-day auction result but has been sold privately for well above one hundred thousand dollars. Why so much? The Democratic Party was pretty broke in 1920. Button makers produced a few sample designs (known as jugates when both candidates are shown), but because of the slightly greater cost of a two-photo button compared to a simple name or slogan button, few local party organizations placed orders, and those placed were small. There are at least six different designs from several different button-making companies but only around fifty known examples of the Cox-Roosevelt jugate.

"With Truman for civil rights": early use of the words *civil rights* on a button

1948 This 1-inch litho tin button reading "With Truman for Civil Rights" is a scarce artifact from Harry Truman's surprise victory over Thomas Dewey in the 1948 presidential election. While a few civil rights–themed buttons date to the early 1900s, including a few issued just after the 1909 founding of the NAACP, Truman's campaign produced at least four different buttons on which the phrase *civil rights* appears. His was the first presidential campaign to produce buttons using those words.

JIMMY HOFFA FOR PRESIDENT TEAMSTERS

1957

What—Me Worry? I'm Voting MAD ALFRED E. NEUMAN FOR PRESIDENT

1960

CAPT. JOHN BIRCH

MAY 28, 1918

AUG. 25, 1945

"First Casualty of W.W. III"

1964

I'M STILL MADLY FOR ADLAI

1956

IN MEMORIAM

MAY 29 1917

NOV. 22 1963

PRESIDENT

JOHN F. KENNEDY

1963

BURN BABY BURN!

1965

5¢ HEAD START

1965

FIFTH AVE. MARCH 26 MASS PROTEST 1966

VIETNAM PEACE PARADE COMMITTEE

1966

What -- Me Worry??

1964

"FATEH" Palestine National Liberation Movement

1965

EASTER 1965

1965

FASLANE COME-ALL-YE 1965

1965

FORGET OXFAM FEED TWIGGY

1967

STRANGER LOVE LIVES

1966

USERS ARE LOSERS

1967

1967

DRAFT BEER NOT BOYS
1967

BATMAN & ROBIN
1966

MELTS IN YOUR MIND NOT IN YOUR HAND
1967

NO VIOLENCIA ES NUESTRA FUERZA
1968

Strike! for high school rights APRIL 15 smc
1967

1967

WE MOURN OUR LOSS 1925 1968 ROBERT F. KENNEDY
1968

NEITHER RED NOR YELLOW I AM TRUE TO USA
1967

I HAVE A DREAM LET FREEDOM RING JAN. 15, 1929 APRIL 4, 1968 A GREAT AMERICAN REV. MARTIN LUTHER KING
1968

HEIL DALEY!
1968

ALLEN GINSBERG FOR PRESIDENT
1968

VOTE PIG Yippie! IN '68
1968

REMEMBER THE PUEBLO!
1968

HUEY NEWTON 7th C.D. FOR CONGRESS
1968

ELDRIDGE CLEAVER FOR PRESIDENT
1968

POOR PEOPLES CAMPAIGN FOR POOR POWER "I have a dream . . ." Rev. Dr. Martin Luther King, Jr.
1968

1967

1966

1964

1968

1968

1967

"Free Speech F.S.M.": an unassuming button symbolizes a tumultuous decade of protest

1964 In September 1964, Katherine Towle, dean of students at the University of California, Berkeley, sent a letter to a full spectrum of off-campus groups registered with her office, from the University Young Republicans to University Friends of the Student Nonviolent Coordinating Committee (SNCC). It decreed that off-campus groups would no longer be permitted to collect money or do anything else to "support or advocate off-campus political action" in "the 26 foot strip of brick walkway at the campus entrance on Bancroft and Telegraph Avenue." Representatives from eighteen student groups met with the dean; despite some compromise, the ban on advocacy, solicitation of donations, and sales of bumper stickers and buttons remained. Defying the ban, the members of the Congress of Racial Equality (CORE) erected a table in front of Sproul Hall, and campus police shortly thereafter arrested CORE activist Jack Weinberg. While police carried Weinberg (who went limp) to a police car, students surrounded the car and deflated its tires. Thirty-two hours later, after chanting, singing, and speeches, most notably by de facto leader Mario Savio from atop the police car, students formed the United Front committee and the university's president, Clark Kerr, signed the Pact of October 2, which ended the sit-in (but not the problems). A few days later, this simple "Free Speech F.S.M." 15/16-inch button was made, documenting the first mass act of civil disobedience on an American college campus in the 1960s— a harbinger of the protest and civil disobedience of the second half of that decade.

HUMPHREY MUSKIE
1968

NIXON AGNEW
1968

YOUTH LIBERATION
1970

McCARTHY'S MILLION
1968

MAGOO
1969

BOYCOTT SCAB GRAPES
1969

Radical Radishes
1969

BUY BUTTONS not bombs
1968

PING-PONG POWER
1972

FLY IT! DON'T BURN IT
1969

YOU FIGHT & DIE BUT CAN'T VOTE AT 18
1969

REGISTER to VOTE DON'T VOTE to REGISTER.
1973

BAN THE BOMBERS
SDS
1971

SKINNY CAT FOR McGOVERN
1972

DR. RON PAUL FOR CONGRESS
1974

FREE JOHN SINCLAIR and all political prisoners
1971

Yippie! *1972*

ERA YES *1974*

SUPPORT THE PRESIDENT! *1974*

Thanks...Jerry *1974*

IMPEACH THE (EXPLETIVE DELETED) *1974*

*Attica ™ *1974*

4th annual christopher street gay pride day . STONEWALL INN '73 *1973*

SUPPORT THE GAY RIGHTS AMENDMENT IN CONGRESS *1975*

1-2-3-4: the chant heard around the world

1967 This fairly scarce 3-inch button repeats, politely, the popular chant of demonstrators: "1-2-3-4, we don't want your f—ing war." The chant was heard worldwide for years, but the button was produced briefly, perhaps for a circa-1967 one-day Vietnam War protest that may have been dampened by rain, as nearly all known examples have a bit of the tan stain caused when moisture rusts the metal behind a button's paper. Surprisingly, Vietnam-related protests date back to 1945, when United States Merchant Marine seamen condemned the US government for allowing US merchant ships to transport French troops to Vietnam to keep their colony subjugated. The accepted dates of the war run from November 1, 1955, to November 30, 1975, when South Vietnam's capital, Saigon, fell to the North. Other popular antiwar slogans appearing on buttons include "Bring the troops home now!" and the anti-draft slogans "Hell, no, we won't go!" and "Girls say yes to boys who say no."

1-2-3-4 W.D.W.Y.F.W.

WIN
WIN WI WIN
WIN WIN WIN WIN
WIN WIN
WIN WIN WIN WIN
WIN WIN WIN
INFLATION
WIN
1974

HARRIS '75
1975

FEET FOR WHAT
MAY 17
1976

WAYNE COUNTY
NOT GUILTY!!!
1977

OUR MUSIC! REGGAE SOUL ROCK 'N' ROLL
ROCK AGAINST RACISM
AND PUNK JAZZ FUNK
1976

WE'VE CARRIED THE RICH FOR 200 YEARS-
JULY 4TH COALITION
LET'S GET THEM OFF OUR BACKS
1976

J.C. CAN SAVE AMERICA
1976

MILK for SUPERVISOR
1977

SPEAK OUT FOR THOSE WHO CAN'T
MARCH FOR SOVIET JEWRY MAY 22
1977

DUMP CARTER
1978

THE DRAFT 1979
Oct 15-16
BERKELEY TO OAKLAND
1979

NORMALIZATION NOW
1978

I ♥ AMERICA
IN SPITE OF
TAXES
PAT. PEND. WANNA ENTERPRISES ROCHESTER NH
1983

DOGS for DISAR-MA-MENT
RAGAMUFFIN Jr.
1983

STOP DIABLO
1979

DON'T KILL PEACE
1984

AMERICAN INDIANS DIED SO THAT YOU CAN EAT HAM BUR GERS
1983

SUPPORT THE REVOLUTION IN PERU
1985

THE GREAT AMERICAN PRESIDENTIAL DEBATE
-VS-
Reagan • Mondale
OCT. 7, 1984
LOUISVILLE, KENTUCKY
1984

CRACK DOWN ON CRACK!
© 1986 THEODORE WHITE
1986

COMPLETE, EXTEND THE REVOLUTION! SMASH U.S. IMPERIALISM!
Defend Nicaragua! Crush the Contras!
SYC
1986

ABOLISH APARTHEID
DIVEST NOW
1983

I Dial for the DUKE
Authorized and paid for by the Dukakis for President Committee, Inc.
1988

AMNESTY INTERNATIONAL
1961 1991
30 YEARS WORKING FOR HUMAN RIGHTS
1991

Enough
© Rostino 88
1988

AIDS ○ TRADING FEARS ○ FOR FACTS
© K. Haring 88
A GUIDE FOR TEENS
Consumer Reports Books
1988

DON'T CALL ME GIRL I AM A WOMAN
1974

PATCHWORK MAJORITY
1975

CALL ME Ms.
1974

YOUTH LIBERATION
1977

BLACK SISTERS UNITE
1974

INTERNATIONAL WOMEN'S DAY
MARCH & RALLY   MARCH 11, 1978
1978

1975 INTERNATIONAL WOMEN'S DAY
MARCH 8
1975

NEVER ANOTHER BATTERED WOMAN
1977

FOR PRESIDENT SHIRLEY CHISHOLM UNBOSSED AND UNBOUGHT FEMINIST PARTY
1972

ELECT THE UNDERACHIEVERS IN '92

1992

VOTE FOR
★ ★ MY DADDY! ★ ★

BILL ★
CLINTON
FOR PRESIDENT

Chelsea Clinton

34

1992

1991

Barbara Boxer
California

SOME
WOMEN
ARE BORN
LEADERS

Lynn Yeakel
Pennsylvania

Carol Moseley Braun
Illinois

Jean Lloyd-Jones
·Iowa

Diane Feinstein
California

1992

Fight
Racism
& Police
Brutality

NATIONAL PEOPLE'S CAMPAIGN

1995

RENEWING AMERICA
TOGETHER

PRESIDENT
GEORGE BUSH

VICE PRESIDENT
DICK CHENEY

2000

FIGHT
DRUGS
WITH
JOBS
NOT
JAILS!

ALL·PEOPLES
CONGRESS

1992

MILLION MAN MARCH

1

IN A
MILLION

OCTOBER 16, 1995 WASHINGTON, D.C.

1995

NO
MORE
SWEATSHOPS!

disneysweatshops.org

2005

STAND FOR CHILDREN 1st
WASHINGTON D.C.
1996

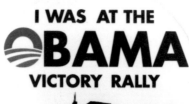

I WAS AT THE OBAMA VICTORY RALLY
NOVEMBER 4TH 2008
GRANT PARK CHICAGO, IL
2008

SKOLSTREJK FÖR KLIMATET
2019

OCCU-PIE 1%
2011

YOUTH CLIMATE STRIKE
2019

MORE THOUGHTS NO MORE PRAYERS — TIME FOR ACTION
2018

2016

Stonewall 50—WorldPride NYC

2019

This 3-inch button from June 2019 marks the fiftieth anniversary of the 1969 Stonewall Inn riots as well as the first time WorldPride was held in the United States. An estimated five million participated in Pride Weekend in Manhattan; four million viewed the twelve-hour Pride March on June 30, with 150,000 preregistered participants.

STONEWALL 50

Events

The earliest button to display a date (to the best of the authors' research) was ordered from Whitehead & Hoag in Newark, New Jersey, by the Indiana State Medical Society for its two-day annual meeting in Fort Wayne, Indiana, held May 28–29, 1896. ● Artists employed by button companies had a great deal of freedom to create attention-grabbing designs promoting events. Clowns, devils, dancing ladies, and cartoon animals proliferated on the earliest buttons made to herald street fairs, carnivals, flower and fruit festivals, Chautauqua assemblies, and harvest celebrations. The earliest World's Fair buttons were made for the 1898 Trans-Mississippi and International Exposition in Omaha, Nebraska, and the earliest Frontier Day button promoted the Cheyenne, Wyoming, rodeo of September 1898. ● Button makers found a year-round market for buttons celebrating secular holidays like July 4, Labor Day, and Mother's Day. Buttons for religious holidays—especially those picturing Santa Claus—were particularly colorful. City centennials, the birthdays of Presidents Washington and Lincoln, and (beginning in the 1950s) winter festivals all brought significant orders to the nation's button makers. ● The political and social turmoil of the 1960s saw the rise of buttons for protest events such as civil rights and anti–Vietnam War marches. The 1970s introduced gay and women's rights demonstrations and Earth Day, and the 1980s added antihunger and antinuclear rallies. In many cases from the past 125 years, a humble button might just be the sole surviving artifact of a significant moment in time.

PEARL DIVING CHAMPIONSHIP 1924

1924

Fiesta de la Luna
CHULA VISTA CALIFORNIA
AUGUST 15-16-17 1947

1947

NEWPORT JAZZ FESTIVAL

1954

I HAVE BEEN THERE
GOING DOWN! MONROE DEC. 28. '05.
MUSKRAT CARNIVAL

1905

J. FLOERSHEIM,
KUNSTADTER & CO.,
JACKSON AND MARKET STS.,
CHICAGO, ILL.
MFD. UNDER PAT. DATES
JULY 17, 1894
APRIL 14, 1896
JULY 21, 1896

Great Chicago Fire: twenty-fifth anniversary

1896

The Great Chicago Fire spanned three days, October 8–10, 1871. Its cause is still officially unknown, but, as this 1¼-inch button shows, blame most often lands on the O'Leary family cow, which kicked over a lantern in a small barn that bordered the alley behind 137 DeKoven Street. This button was made to mark October 9, 1896, as "Chicago Day," coinciding with the twenty-fifth anniversary of the fire. It also called attention to a "Sound Money Demonstration," a rally for William McKinley's presidential campaign. Of interest to button geeks, the text on the back paper proves beyond a doubt that the process of making pin-back buttons, then only ten months old at the most, was already being licensed to other companies by Whitehead & Hoag: "J. Floersheim, Kunstadter & Co., Jackson and Market Sts., Chicago, Ill. Mfd. Under Pat. Dates July 17, 1894 / April 14, 1896 / July 21, 1896." The three patent dates are those belonging to W&H; the final date of July 21 could be regarded as the birthday of the pin-back button.

Announcement for "The Doctors": the earliest known dated button

A person associated with the Indiana State Medical Society somehow knew that Whitehead & Hoag, based in Newark, New Jersey, had just started making pin-back buttons and ordered this "May 28 & 29, 1896 Annual Meeting" ⅞-inch button with a blank back paper. The local *Fort Wayne News*, under the headline "The Doctors," reported on the convention's first day of activities. This was the group's forty-seventh annual meeting, held at Plymouth Congregational Church, with over one hundred delegates. The pulpit, "decorated by Miss Flick," was banked ten feet high, with palms interspersed with potted plants and carnations. The convention was called to order by group president Dr. Miles F. Porter, followed by a welcoming address by Mayor Scherer. (The report makes no mention of the button.) The second known dated button, with a back paper naming W&H as the maker and including the company's patent dates, is another ⅞-inch button picturing the Fayette Country, Pennsylvania, courthouse (built 1892), with surrounding text "Uniontown Centennial July 4, 1896." The authors challenge anyone to find a button dated on its face earlier than May 28, 1896.

FORT WAYNE CARNIVAL AND STREET FAIR

Oct. 4, 5, 6, 7, 1898.

1898

THE TURLOCK MELON CARNIVAL

AUG. 24 AND 25.

1914

KANSAS KARNIVAL KREW

OCT. 4-5-6-7, 1898.

K K

K

KANSAS CITY.

1898

MEET ME AT THE SACRAMENTO FREE STREET FAIR & TRADES CARNIVAL

A WEEK OF UNALLOYED JOY

APRIL 30TH TO MAY 5TH 1900.

1900

1917

1909

1898

1911

The Collision:
"The great machines, snorting and groaning under the pressure of steam, seemed to invite attack"

ca. 1905 So wrote an anonymous reporter for the Louisville, Kentucky, *Courier-Journal* of September 24, 1902. This 1¼-inch "See the Collision" button is a rare souvenir from an early twentieth-century spectator sport usually held at fairgrounds. Professional promoters would acquire two massive steam locomotives, past their prime but functional, and employ them in a head-on demolition derby. Well promoted and held late in the day to allow the crowd to build, the spectacle positioned the two behemoths at opposite ends of some two thousand feet of track. From their respective cabs, the daring engineers would signal for a simultaneous start, open their throttles, build speed toward forty miles per hour, and, seconds from disaster, jump for their lives. The ensuing explosion of steam and steel was a guaranteed crowd-pleaser, although promoters often had difficulty keeping crowds of thirty-five thousand or so far enough away from the impact site to avoid the shower of shrapnel and flying debris. At this event, the *Courier-Journal* reporter noted: "No one in the crowd was heard to complain."

Wyoming's Frontier Day: the real photo button

1898 The first Frontier Day celebration in Cheyenne, Wyoming, was a one-day event held in 1897. Its pony races, steer roping, and bronco busting were so popular that the next year's festival, which this 1¼-inch button commemorates, was expanded to two days (although the button still uses "Day") plus a Labor Day parade. While the 1896 presidential campaign buttons of William McKinley and William Jennings Bryan had featured photographic portraits of the two candidates, real photo buttons picturing any other subject had been a rarity in 1896, barely in use in 1897, and only finally gained some traction in 1898. The term *real photo* indicates an image printed on photographic paper, as opposed to one "screened" with tiny dots and printed on a printing press. The result, produced in either a high-contrast tonal range or a broad, graduated range of sepia or black-and-white tones, is an exceptionally sharp, highly detailed image. Buttons produced in this manner were typically made in relatively small quantities because of the labor and time investment, and often carry neither a back paper nor text identifying the maker. Other 1898 real photo buttons include one for the strongman Eugen Sandow (see page 124); one for the Coldwater, Michigan, Queen of the Carnival (see page 76); and several for America's hero of the year, Admiral George Dewey of Spanish-American War fame (see page 175).

...and speaking of Admiral Dewey

1898 On Labor Day 1898 (the very same Monday as Wyoming's Frontier Day parade), folks in Minneapolis headed out the door wearing a "Good Everywhere" button that served as their ticket to the five-day "Festival of Fire." Less than three years earlier, Wilhelm Röntgen had discovered X-rays (*X* for *unknown*). His December 1895 radiograph of his wife's left hand, showing the bones with a wedding band around one finger, quickly transformed medicine. Drawing on the wonder of X-ray imagery and the novelty of the newfangled pin-back serving as an admission ticket, some creative Festival of Fire committee member composed this design. The event was held in conjunction with the Minnesota State Fair and was inspired by the United States' recent and exceedingly fast victory over Spain in the Spanish-American War. Featured were huge parades of military units and Civil War veterans, with exhibits of war artifacts from Santiago, Cuba, and Cavite, in the Philippines. The Festival of Fire turned into a big fireworks display on closing day. Only two known ticket buttons survive.

NATIONAL CORN HUSKING CONTEST

NORTON, KANSAS
Nov. 14, 1930

1930

MACON COUNTY CORN CARNIVAL

DECATUR, ILL.
OCT. 26, 27, 28 & 29.

1898

CORN AND ALFALFA EXPOSITION
BENSON, MINN.
NOV. 26-28. 1914

1914

DECATUR CORN CARNIVAL AND EXPOSITION

DECATUR, ILL., OCT. 17, 18, 19, 20 & 21, '99

1899

WICHITA'S STREET FAIR & CARNIVAL.
OCT. 16 TO 21.

1899.

1899

Funny Hat Night at Long Beach

Nov. 30, — 1911.

783

1911

Ukiah
SEPT 18,
1915

1915

NATIONAL THRIFT WEEK
JANUARY 17-24. 1921

1921

PANAMA CALIFORNIA INTERNATIONAL EXPOSITION

I PAID
DEDICATION DAY
SATURDAY
MARCH 18
OFFICIAL SOUVENIR
ADMIT ONE
SAN DIEGO
1916

1916

1933
A CENTURY
OF PROGRESS
CHICAGO

1933

Oh, Boy!
Some
Outing
D.P.&S.
Carsonia
Park
Aug. 27, 1920

1920

A happy
New Year.

SOUVENIR OF
Butcher's Association
SUMMER'S PARADE
LANCASTER, PA. JAN. 1. 1913

1913

WARM MITT SOCIETY
OF THE GREAT LAKES
1916
1st ANNUAL MITT FEST

1916

COME TO TOYLAND AT FOSTER & COCHRAN'S

1913

SEMI-CENTENNIAL
JUNE 24-25-26
BATTLE LITTLE BIG HORN

1926

19 28
BOYS' WEEK

1928

I WAS
THERE

1939

JULY FOURTH
1925

1925

MERRY XMAS
SPREAD THE NEWS
GOOD-BY BLUES
1932
HAPPY
NEW YEAR

1932

I SAW BUCK ROGERS
25th CENTURY SHOW
DID YOU
A CENTURY OF PROGRESS

1934

NATIONAL SCHOOL MUSIC COMPETITION FESTIVAL

REGION NINE

COLORADO SPRINGS, MAY 11-12-13, 1939

1939

WISCONSIN
VS
CHICAGO
19 36
HOMECOMING
WELCOME

1936

FIFTEENTH ANNUAL COWBOY BALL
DANCE, COWBOY, DANCE!
LAMAR, COLO., DEC. 27, 1935

1935

GOLDEN ANNIVERSARY
1898-NABISCO-1948
NATIONAL BISCUIT
COMPANY

1948

NORTHLAND MARDI GRAS

Ladysmith, Wis.
July 20-22
1951

1951

NUDIST CONTEST

1934

G·V·PARK
Water
Carnival

AUGUST 13, 1921

1921

NEW YORK WORLD'S FAIR
1939

LET'S GO!

"ASBURY PARK DAY"
THURSDAY
MAY 18th

1939

Keeping it simple: just "BE"

1967 The four organizers of the first Central Park Be-In, held on Easter Sunday, March 26, 1967, had a $250 budget that covered three thousand posters, forty thousand handouts in psychedelic colors designed by and carrying the now-iconic name of Peter Max, and an undocumented but small number of 1¼-inch buttons with the place, date, and "BE" boldly printed. An estimated ten thousand participants picnicked, chanted, and generally frolicked in Sheep Meadow. And yes, there was some perfectly legal smoking of banana peels. The police profile was low, and a few small skirmishes were contained. Monday's *Daily News* headline was "Strangest Beings Attend Be-In in Central Park." The *New York Times* described Bronx poets, East Village dropouts, East Side interior decorators, West Side teachers, and Long Island teenyboppers wearing "carnation petals and paper stars and tiny mirrors on their foreheads, paint around the mouth and cheeks, flowering bed sheets, buttons, and tights." The following year, in 1968, a peace rally and the Easter Be-In were combined, swelling the crowd to ninety thousand. In place of her husband, Dr. Martin Luther King Jr., who had been assassinated ten days earlier, Coretta Scott King spoke, declaring, "The interrelatedness of domestic and foreign affairs is no longer questioned."

I'm Joining...
HANDS ACROSS AMERICA
May 25, 1986

Coca-Cola

In Association with The Coca-Cola Company

1986

·LESBIAN·GAY·CHRISTOPHER·St·LIBERATION·

JUNE·26·83·NEW·YORK·

1983

THE GREAT PEACE 1986 MARCH

1986

NATIONAL COMING OUT DAY...

OCTOBER 11

1988

Caroline's 7th Birthday

2014

I WAS THERE!
NATIONAL MUSEUM of AFRICAN AMERICAN HISTORY & CULTURE
DEDICATION DAY 9/24/2016

2016

KUJICHAGULIA · UJIMA · UJAMAA · UMOJA · NIA · KUUMBA · IMANI

DEC. 26

JAN. 1

KWANZAA

1984

COLUMBUS QUINCENTENNIAL

1492 - 1992

1992

THIS BUTTON CELEBRATES THE 116TH BIRTHDAY OF THE PIN-BACK BUTTON
NATIONAL PIN-BACK BUTTON DAY 2012
PATENT #564,356 on JULY 21 1896

2012

REMEMBER 911

2001

Icebreakers

All buttons are conversation starters, but these novelty buttons have little other reason to exist. These facilitators of human interaction might be worn by the person sitting next to you who wants to tell you a joke or just strike up some small talk. Mostly, they're humorous, showing what people found funny in their day. Some are public service announcements or points of pride, while others just try to stir interest. ● From the 1920s to the 1950s, Johnson Smith and Co. produced all sorts of funny, if questionable, buttons with sayings. Many are just text with a checkered or solid border; some tell, by rebus, a variation of "Confucius Say…" followed by a shocking political statement or an announcement that the wearer is looking for love. ● The 1960s brought a new style of humor—gift and head shops sold an array of countercultural messages. Mostly text, they often made light of sexuality and drugs. Since buttons were so widely worn during the 1960s and '70s, there were also many self-referential designs, such as "Don't you feel like a nut reading a button with no message?" ● The 1970s saw the heyday of streaking buttons—1974 was the year when a streaker crossed the stage at the Academy Awards and the Ray Stevens song "The Streak" was a number one hit (see page 100; the question remains as to where the buttons were worn). ● The 1980s and '90s saw a profusion of funny buttons. Often bought at the mall or a novelty gift shop, these buttons allowed people to express snotty humor without saying a word. Jokes involved farting, nose picking, bitching, being old—anything to get a lighthearted response. In the 1999 movie *Office Space*, waiters for a national food chain are required to wear a certain amount of "flair" in the form of joke buttons. It wasn't the finest hour for buttons—they are portrayed as dehumanizing—but still, they provide a significant cultural reference point.

23 skidoo: snappy slogans delivered to your doorstep

ca. 1914 Johnson Smith and Co., purveyor of all things enticing since 1914, sold buttons in its mail order catalog among the mini bonsai gardens, BB guns, fake vomit, and other novelties. The company used a few standard templates, updating the buttons' text for each new design in an effort to provide engaging, up-to-date humor. Around the turn of the twentieth century, "23 skidoo" (meaning "Get outta here!" or "Scram!") was one of the most popular slang terms. While its origin is disputed, the expression is often associated with the sidewalk outside the Flatiron Building at East Twenty-Third Street in Manhattan. The building's signature shape created wind currents that lifted women's skirts as they turned the corner. Men would line up against the building to catch a glimpse of a woman's exposed ankle but would often be "23 skidoo'ed" by police who knew what was up. The 1901 film short *What Happened on Twenty-Third Street, New York City* shows such a moment. The scene was cited as an inspiration for the iconic sequence in *The Seven Year Itch* when Marilyn Monroe's skirt is raised by the air from a subway grate.

FRIENDS
DON'T
LET FRIENDS
DRIVE
DRUNK

1983

IT'S
A PLEASURE
TO HAVE A FRIEND
LIKE YOU

1912

TO-MORROW,
TO-DAY WILL BE
YESTERDAY

1912

THIS
BUTTON IS
JUST AN ATTEMPT
TO
COMMUNICATE

1967

CLEANED AND FILLED 100%
1928

I'VE JOINED
1933

UNEMPLOYED SELLING THE DAILY TIMES 2¢ LEND-A-HAND
1931

AT YOUR DOOR
1930

TO FALL IN LOVE IS AWFULLY SIMPLE TO FALL OUT OF IT IS SIMPLY AWFUL
1921

EAT ME AT BREMEN, KANS. JUNE-9-1935
1935

CHILDREN'S SCIENCE FAIR EXHIBITOR 1933
1933

I Have Visited The Gerber Baby
1938

NO! I WILL NOT PAY INFLATION PRICES
1947

YOU CAN'T CARVE A TURKEY with a WOODEN SWORD! ASK ME ...
1936

I SAW GENE AUTRY NOV. 1-11 BOSTON GARDEN RODEO
1940

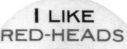

I LIKE RED-HEADS DO YOU?
1945

TIME FOR A CHANGE I LIKE IKE
1952

I AM HELPING PREVENT FOREST FIRES
1947

LET'S BE FRIENDS Sunbeam Bread
1950

ASK ME HOW YOU CAN BE A Quiz Kid
1940

I LIKE STEVENSON
1950

OFFICIAL JETS Red Ball JUNIOR SPACE COMMANDER
1952

I'M ONE COOL CAT AN' THAT IS THAT
1955

IT'S NOT MY FACE - IT'S MY FIGURE
1947

WJBK-TV'S PiRATE PETE FIRST MATE

1954

ANNIE OAKLEY AND TAGG
GAIL DAVIS
MEMBER
SHARPSHOOTER

1954

I'D LIKE TO, BUT I'M IN ANALYSIS

1959

I WAS THERE NEW YORK CITY CONVENTION
BIB LE
JULY 19 TO 26 1953
JEHOVAH'S WITNESSES

1953

I GO POGO

©1956 WALT KELLY

1956

I AM A CAPTAIN KANGAROO KID

1956

I HAVE
Figueroa's
ONE ON

1954

ZD
STRIVE FOR ZERO DEFECTS

1960

MEMBER OF
shay
FUN CLUB

1963

OFFICIAL BADGE
ROCKET POGO STICK CLUB OF NORTH AMERICA

1957

Authorized by THE SMOTHERS BROTHERS &
I AM A FOLK SINGER
Mercury RECORDS

1962

JUNIOR
ASTRONAUTS

1961

WATTS COOKING
WE WANT WORK

1965

LET'S DO THE TWIST

1960

I VISITED BOZO'S CIRCUS
WGN TV
CHANNEL 9

1967

WHEN IT COMES TO BEING WELL STACKED

1967

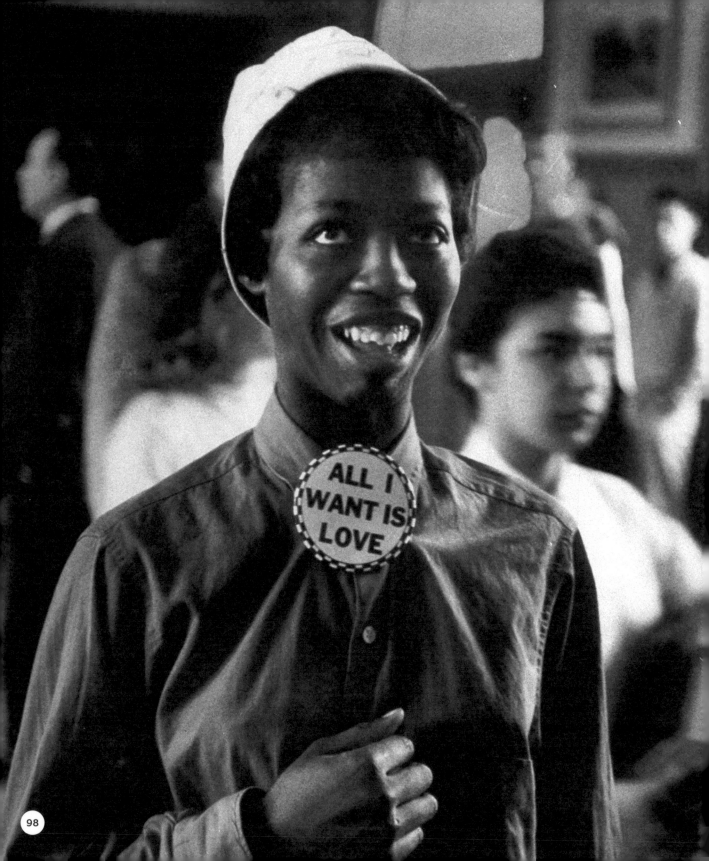

JESUS FREAK

1968

Caution Cigarette Smoking
May Be Hazardous
To Your Health

1967

why
do we kill people
who kill people
to show that
killing people
is wrong ?

1977

DON'T SMOKE DAD

IT MAKES ME SAD

1972

WE'RE MAD AS HELL,
WE'RE NOT GOING TO
TAKE IT ANY MORE.

1977

HANG
IN
THERE,
BABY!

1975

WE
ALL
LIVE IN
HARRISBURG

1979

TO GNOME IS TO LOVE ME

1978

I'm
Ready
For The
80's

1979

I
LIKE
MEAT
LOAF

1990

HAVE A NICE
FOREVER

1982

I GAVE TO
AFRO-
AMERICAN
DAY
1979

1979

PLAYBOY.

1979

ATOMIC POWER?
NO THANK YOU

1980

OFFICIAL
STREAKER

1974

BIG MAC™

KEEPS ME COMING BACK

1979

Smiley face: spreading happiness in a dark time

ca. 1967

In 1963, the smiley face design was created in ten minutes by Harvey Ball, a graphic designer in Worcester, Massachusetts. That simple graphic, intended to improve morale at a life insurance company, became one of the world's most iconic images. Thanks to its circular shape and graphic simplicity, the image works perfectly on a button. To date, over fifty million smiley face buttons have been made, along with countless knockoffs and variations on the theme. Though the design itself is simple, the message behind it can be ambiguous; its vapid quality can convey a sense of false consciousness. In the 1970s, it was an antidote to the grim realities of the Vietnam War. In the 1980s, it became the symbol for rave/acid house culture, and today it has many moods, as depicted in emojis.

The waiter from hell: humor buttons

1980s

Offbeat and offensive buttons were popular in the 1980s. During this era, an abundance of witty sayings, puns, and satirical phrases were conceived and pressed into buttons that were sold at record and gift shops (mostly at the malls). Companies like Button-Up, Sky Ent., and Ephemera, Inc. would invent slogans like "Why Be Normal?" and "Waiter from Hell" for people to wear (anti)socially and proudly. In 1980, Ed Polish and Jeff Errick of Ephemera, Inc., looking for an outlet to piss off the mainstream, found buttons. They made a business out of turning their irreverent humor into something easy to wear. "Eat McShit and Die" was one of their first buttons. Ephemera is still in business and has produced well over five thousand designs. These fun-to-collect buttons were the predecessors of the memes and tweets of our time. They reflect their own time and preserve trends, characters, and sayings that might have otherwise been lost to history: Valley Girl speak ("Gag me with a spoon!"), Dana Carvey's Church Lady from *Saturday Night Live* ("Isn't that special?"), or feelings about incoming technologies ("Did you fart or is that a weird beeper?").

WAITER FROM HELL

PROUDLY SERVING MY CORPORATE MASTERS 1986

SPUDS GORBACHEV *The Communist Party Animal* 1988

I STAND WITH PLANNED PARENTHOOD #StandwithPP 2015

the Moral Majority is Neither 1981

ASK ME ABOUT GRAPHIC NOVELS 1990

GOD Protect Me From Your Followers 2015

reading is sexy 2008

YES WE CODE 2012

DO THE RIGHT THING... GET A MAMMOGRAM 1991

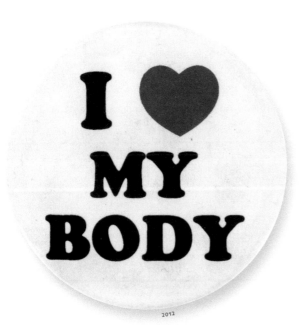

I ♥ MY BODY

2012

I HELPED MAKE LESBIAN, BI & GAY HISTORY

APRIL 25, 1993

WASHINGTON D.C.

1993

I ♥ THE EARTH

April 22, 1990

1990

LOVE ♥ WINS

2015

Nature

The natural world is a perennial subject of buttons: some glorify the beauty of nature and others fight to protect it. Some of the most charming and delicate button graphics are those that represent flowers and fruits. These still lifes reflect a time when the United States was more widely agrarian, around the turn of the twentieth century. ● One simply designed 3-D button reproduces a rose using the technology of the day. The button's metal shell was stamped in the shape of a rose and covered with printed celluloid, giving the petals and leaves a striking, luminescent brightness. This type of button is called Crystoglas; only a few designs were ever made with this technique. ● After the Industrial Revolution, efforts to protect animals and our environment gained momentum. The ASPCA (American Society for the Prevention of Cruelty to Animals) formed in 1866 to advocate for the rights of animals. Band of Mercy organizations formed locally across the nation, with each new member given a button upon joining. In the 1950s, souvenir buttons with images of zoo animals show how we brought the natural world to us. In the 1970s, buttons were used for more specific causes, as activists fought for water conservation, recycling, and myriad other ways to save the Earth. ● With the craft boom of the early 2000s, nature again became a popular source of imagery for buttons and other handcrafted items, summed up by the television show *Portlandia*'s affectionate dig at the crafting movement: "Put a bird on it."

EL DORADO CO. BARTLETT PEAR SHOW
PLACERVILLE, CAL., AUG. 28-30, 1913

NEW YORK STATE FRUIT GROWERS ASSOCIATION
1911

WESTERN NEW YORK
1855   1912
HORTICULTURAL SOCIETY

PRUNE & APRICOT EXPOSITION
Souvenir
SEPT. 21-22 1917
MOUNTAIN VIEW

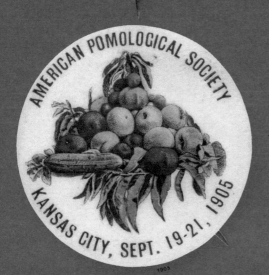

AMERICAN POMOLOGICAL SOCIETY
KANSAS CITY, SEPT. 19-21, 1905

NATIONAL APPLE SHOW
SPOKANE • CHICAGO •
NOV. 14-19 • NOV. 28-DEC. 4

The Audubon Society: the first bird button

ca. 1899

John James Audubon was an American naturalist, ornithologist, and painter who documented American birds in the first half of the nineteenth century. In the second half of that century, millions of waterbirds were killed to decorate hats and other garments with their feathers. In 1896, Harriet Hemenway and Minna B. Hall established the Massachusetts Audubon Society and set out to stop the massacre. By 1898, fifteen additional states and the District of Columbia had state-level organizations. The first of the fifty or so buttons issued with the Audubon Society name during the twentieth century is ⅞ inch and carries a Whitehead & Hoag back paper that was used only in 1898–99. The National Audubon Society was formed in 1905. In 2010, a copy of Audubon's book *The Birds of America* sold at auction for $11.5 million, making those hundred-year-old Audubon buttons sold at the flea market a bargain at the typical ten to twenty dollars.

Charlie Chirp: protector-in-chief

1936

This 1⅝-inch-wide oval has text on the side edge of the button (known as the curl) identifying the issuer as "French's Bird Seed and Biscuit / R.T. French Co., Rochester, N.Y." Depicted is Charlie Chirp, a bright yellow canary with policeman's hat, pipe in beak, badge on breast, and gun belt at waist. Charlie was identified in French's advertising around 1936 as "Charlie Chirp Canary Detective." Produced as a pin-back button as well as one with two slotted tabs cut into a metal back, this was a giveaway to fans who sent the name of their own canary (with required coupon and coin to cover postage) to be placed on a personalized oval. Those with the slotted back were designed to be fastened to the canary's cage for display (and to ward off danger). In addition to the buttons pictured here, Teeney, Snippy, and Gale have briefly come to market on eBay and now reside in locations unknown.

"Swat the fly": buttons take on public health

(ca. 1911) The fly-eradication movement in the United States kicked off around 1909 and peaked in the years 1925 to 1935. Most of the half dozen or so different buttons related to this subject, like these 1¼-inch and ⅞-inch examples, seem to be from around 1910 to 1920. As the Richmond, Indiana, newspaper reported on March 19, 1915: "Thousands of human lives are sacrificed annually because no method has been devised for abolishing the fly." The importance of keeping flies away from food supplies was publicized through posters, newspaper articles, direct mail, and buttons. Each spring brought renewed efforts, as entomologists emphasized that it was easier to keep the pests from increasing in the spring than to reduce their number in the summer.

"Meet Blinky": the one-eyed alligator

1970 In the early 1970s, Lakeland, Florida, about halfway between Tampa and Orlando, had an overfriendly alligator. This 1½-inch button, probably financed by the local chamber of commerce, takes some creative license by portraying him with an eye patch, but Blinky was indeed a one-eyed gator; in fact, the *Lakeland Ledger* said in 2003 that he was also missing a foot. Humans led to Blinky's undoing when they began enticing him with food out of the safety of Lake Mirror. The Lakeland Parks and Recreation director, Bob Donahay, observed that Blinky "eventually got too friendly....Anytime it saw people, it would come out on shore like a pet dog." Local officials recognized an accident waiting to happen; mascot or not, Blinky found himself relocated to Homosassa Springs Wildlife State Park, where Jake, the park's resident large and healthy crocodile, eventually attacked and killed him. Meanwhile, Blinky continues to be memorialized in Lakeland by both a realistic sculpture and a more abstract one made of mechanical metal junk parts known as "Mecha-Blinky," which sits in the grass on the north side of Blinky's former home.

The first Earth Day: Philadelphia's button

1970

Rachel Carson's 1962 best seller *Silent Spring* started a groundswell of opposition to the poisoning of the Earth and its occupants. As awareness of our pressing ecological problems grew, Wisconsin senator Gaylord Nelson proposed Earth Day as a national day of observance. What was called "Earth Week" originated in Philadelphia, with events and speakers that culminated in the first Earth Day on April 22, 1970. The event drew twenty million Americans to coast-to-coast rallies. Nationwide, small groups fighting local battles discovered other, similar groups with common values; that synergy helped fuel the environmental movement, with 2020 marking the fiftieth anniversary of Earth Day. The first Earth Week committee selected a design by David Powell for its official button, a 1⅜-inch lithograph produced by Horn Badge Co. in Glenside, Pennsylvania.

Mobilization for animals

1983

The twentieth-century revolution in human rights accelerated in the 1960s. Although less publicized, the 1960s and '70s also saw progress on the animal rights front. A landmark was the publication of Peter Singer's book *Animal Liberation* in 1975 and the quick rise of the militant Animal Liberation Front in Britain and the United States. Another milestone, documented by this 1¾-inch button, occurred on April 24, 1983, when the advocacy group Mobilization for Animals held protest rallies in four US cities and ten overseas countries at institutions or companies engaged in primate research or breeding programs. The 1980s produced a particularly striking array of not only animal rights buttons but also numerous other well-designed, eye-catching buttons promoting all types of environmental causes.

Organizations

Humans need to feel a sense of belonging, and buttons can help like-minded people find each other or identify as members of a group. ● Some of the most intricate and clever buttons were made for Elks and Shiners fraternal groups in Troy, New York. They featured an elk or a camel wearing the products of the International Shirt & Collar Co. ● Buttons identified professional groups like women lawyers, firefighters, and poultry farmers. Unions would give workers buttons designating specific months, proving that they had paid their dues (a practice that continues today). ● Many social movements have used buttons; some have been fastidious, like a 1919 example for the "Do Without Club," which advocated against using slang. Others have promoted civil rights, like buttons produced by the NAACP (National Association for the Advancement of Colored People) as part of an anti-lynching campaign. And the WPU (Women's Social and Political Union), a group of suffragists, came together wearing buttons emblazoned with the rallying cry "Deeds Not Words." ● Phony organizations were sometimes invented to encourage desirable behavior in children. Starting in the 1930s, kids might receive buttons for having good hygiene, teeth, or posture. If they were compliant at the dentist, they could earn an "I Can Take It" button, or if they ate all their food, they could be in the "Clean Plate Club."

"Bound for Washington: from the hot sands of Florida"

1900

Freemasonry began in medieval times but was first formalized in a fraternal society in London in 1717. In 1870, two New York City Freemasons came up with the idea of an offshoot fraternity that would emphasize fun along with fellowship. They created rituals, emblems, symbols, and costumes based on Middle Eastern themes, with group headquarters called temples. The first such was Mecca Temple, established at Masonic Hall in New York City on September 26, 1872. Growth was slow but took off in the 1890s. By the time this 1¾-inch button was designed for the Jacksonville, Florida, Morocco Temple contingent to the 1900 Washington, DC, convention, dubbed the "Imperial Session," there were fifty-five thousand members in eighty-two temples. All eighty-two were represented in a May 22 parade reviewed by President William McKinley. No longer called the Ancient Arabic Order of the Nobles of the Mystic Shrine, today some 196 chapters with 350,000 members are known as Shriners International.

LAKOTA WHITE FLYERS
22ND ANNUAL TOURNAMENT JAMESTOWN N.D. JUNE 13·14· and 15. 1905.
1905

All Going To Great AFRICAN METHODIST E., A·L., & M. CONVENTION LITTLE ROCK JULY 10, 11, 12, 1906. WILL "U" B THERE?
1906

Y. M. C. A.
SEPTEMBER 5, 1903
1903

MEET ME AT S.E.K.T.A. Nov. 29–Dec. 1, 1906. PARSONS, KANS.
1906

I.O.O.B. WE LIVE TO STING
1906

DEFIANCE POULTRY AND PET STOCK ASSOCIATION DEFIANCE OHIO
1907

OLD STUDENTS OF ST. JOHN'S RE·UNION 1907
1907

ASCALON COMMANDERY KNIGHTS TEMPLAR No 59 BELONG TO ASCALON, WHERE YOU FROM? YOU SHOULD BELONG TO ASCALON PITTSBURGH PA, 1906.
1906

NEW YORK WOMEN'S LEAGUE FOR ANIMALS
1910

I HEAR ME CROW AT LITITZ DEC. 27-09 TO JAN 1·10
1910

CALIFORNIA STATE SPIRITUALIST ASS'N.
1915

WEST VIRGINIA BOYS AND GIRLS AGRICULTURAL CLUB
1913
1913

CONNECTICUT WOMEN'S LEAGUE FOR ANIMALS
1914

Maurice L. Rothschild & Co. is helping PULL FOR PLAYGROUNDS INSTITUTE SESSION open to public THURSDAY EVE APRIL 6 WATCH THE PAPERS
1911

KANSAS SHOE RETAILER'S ASS'N. TOPEKA FEB. 26·27·28·1914.
1914

N.Y. STATE TEACHERS ASS'N. SYRACUSE, N.Y. NOV. 24·26, 1913. CLINTON SQUARE
1913

OVER THE TOP
1918

BOMBERETTES
1918

CITIZENS COMMITTEE OF CONEY ISLAND
1910

NEWARK BOY SCOUTS
1915

FIRST COLORED WESLEY CHURCH CHOIR
1921

REMEMBER THE ORPHANS EV. LUTH. ST. JOHN'S ORPHAN'S HOME SULPHUR SPRINGS
1912

HOME GUARDS
1918

TOOTH BRUSH CLUB
1919

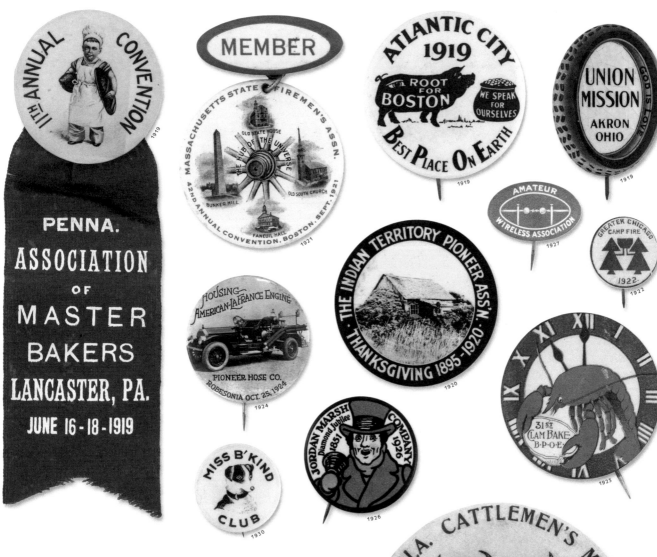

The Oklahoma Cattlemen's Meet: all dressed up

1905 — Two years before Oklahoma achieved statehood in 1907, members of the Oklahoma Live Stock Association assembled in Guthrie to celebrate the tenth anniversary of their organization with their largest convention to date. Coverage extended to Walla Walla, Washington, with the *Evening Times* reporting, "Prominent cattlemen from all sections filled the hall today" and "The business sessions will be interspersed with numerous features of entertainment provided by the citizens of Guthrie." Presumably a good time was had by all (except, in the end, the happy cow couple on this rare 1¾-inch button).

National Committee for a Sane Nuclear Policy (SANE): protesting an existential threat

1958

The world entered the nuclear age at 5:29 AM on July 16, 1945, with a bomb test in the New Mexico desert code-named "Trinity," part of the Manhattan Project. Less than a month later, the United States exploded atomic bombs, first over Hiroshima and then Nagasaki. Japan surrendered on September 2, 1945, and World War II was over. However, the United States continued nuclear testing, joined by Russia and Great Britain. Suddenly, cows eating grass contaminated by radioactive fallout were producing strontium-90-laced milk. In June 1957, twenty-seven citizens concerned by nuclear fallout met in New York City to form an action committee. They ran a full-page ad in the *New York Times* that read: "We Are Facing a Danger Unlike Any Danger That Has Ever Existed." By summer 1958, the era of this 1¼-inch button, SANE had 130 chapters and some 25,000 American members. In the 1980s, SANE joined with the Nuclear Weapons Freeze Campaign, and in 1993 they adopted the name Peace Action. Their goal remains to live without the threat of nuclear weapons.

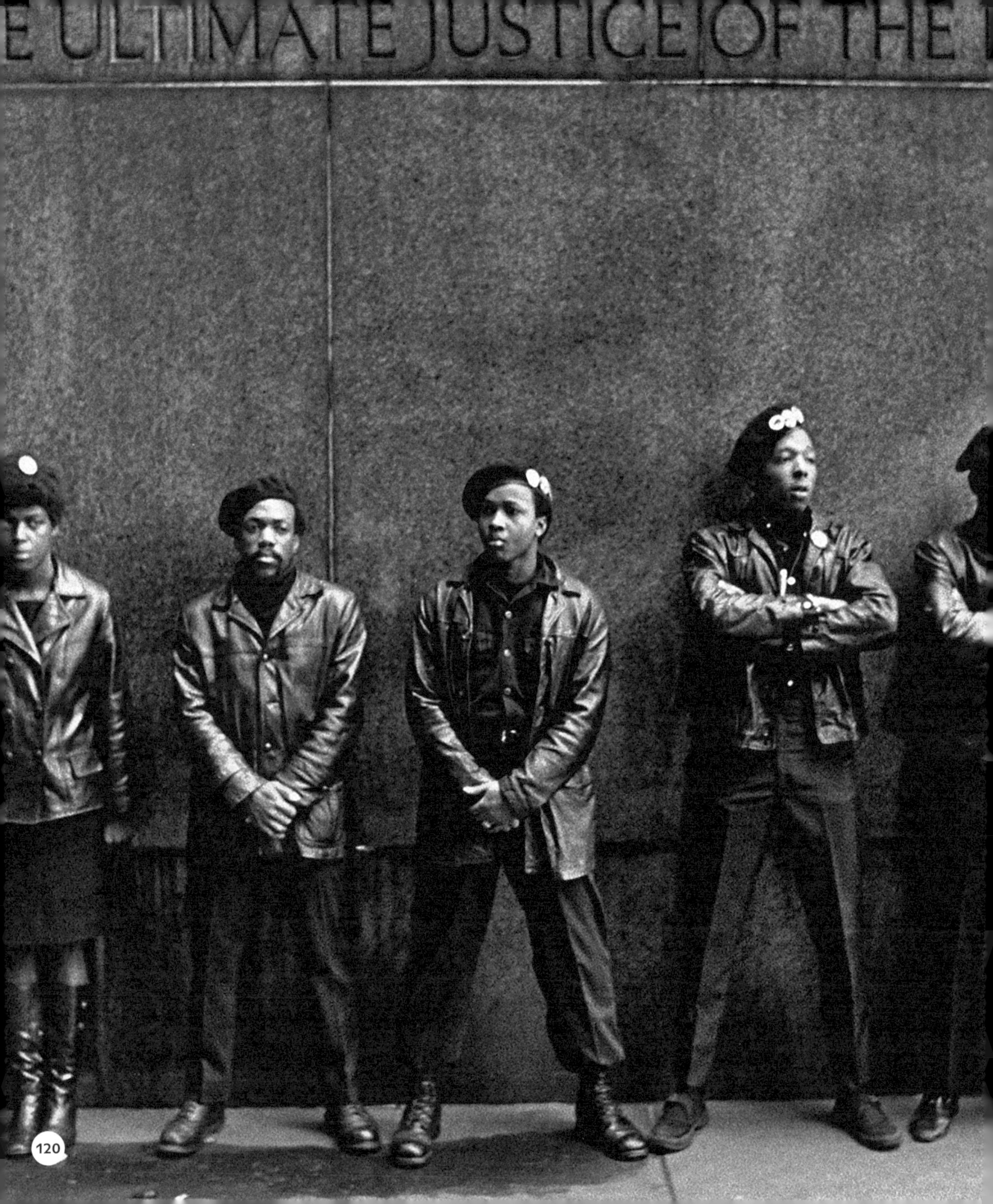
E ULTIMATE JUSTICE OF THE

American Political Items Collectors: button collectors unite

1964

The American Political Items Collectors (APIC) is a nonprofit organization founded in 1945 to encourage the collection and preservation of political campaign memorabilia. The group's interests encompass all types of artifacts, with buttons the leading category. A specialty chapter in APIC is devoted to popular culture buttons, and all types of buttons proliferate at APIC shows nationwide.

People

Wearing buttons with images of notable people celebrates human values, relationships, and connectedness. Each person depicted on these buttons has had enough cultural influence that we consider their actions, ideas, or words to be of value. ● A button depicting George Washington with an ax and cherries conjures up the importance of honesty while bolstering national identity. Someone wearing a button of Queen Victoria is figuratively rubbing elbows with royalty. An image of Robert Peary and Frederick Cook above their respective ships at the North Pole glorifies humanity's quest to conquer the natural world. Buttons of the silent-movie actress Mary Pickford helped make her America's first movie celebrity, and a James Brown button shows admiration for his ingenuity in music and black pride. We can continue to carry the torch of Fannie Lou Hamer, Southern voting and economic activist. Buttons featuring people allow their wearers to literally stand behind the fellow humans they admire.

1897

1906

1909

1910

Marilyn

1955

CASSIUS CLAY

1964

JAMES DEAN

1955

1976

Geronimo: medicine man from the Bedonkohe Band of the Apache Tribe

1899 This 1¼-inch button depicts Geronimo (1829–1909), who spent most of his life resisting both Mexican and American occupation of Apache lands. From 1876 to 1886, Geronimo "surrendered" three times and accepted life on an Apache reservation in Arizona. However, he and his followers staged three breakouts to resume a nomadic life that included raiding settlements in Mexico and the southwestern United States. Captured for the last time in 1886, Geronimo became a prisoner of war under General Nelson Miles and was sent to Florida to join the rest of the exiled Chiricahua tribe of Apaches (thus avoiding Arizona state authorities, who wanted to execute him). At Fort Pickens in Pensacola, Florida, Geronimo became a tourist attraction. He traveled under army guard to the 1898 Trans-Mississippi and International Exposition in Omaha; to the Phoenix Carnival, as shown on this 1899 button; and to the 1901 and 1904 World's Fairs in Buffalo and St. Louis. Geronimo appeared in Pawnee Bill's Wild West Show and in President Theodore Roosevelt's 1905 inaugural parade, riding horseback down Pennsylvania Avenue. He died in 1909 at the Fort Sill Oklahoma Hospital, still a prisoner of war.

Brother Brigham, founder of Salt Lake City

1897

This 1¼-inch button was made for the Utah Pioneer Jubilee held in Salt Lake City July 20–24, 1897. The event celebrated the arrival, fifty years previously, of 1,949 pioneers to what would become the state of Utah. Of that original group, 663 attended the anniversary celebration. The button pictures the pioneers' leader, Brigham Young (1801–1877), founder of Salt Lake City and the second president of the Church of Jesus Christ of Latter-day Saints. Curiously, this rare item is the one and only Mormon-related button the authors have encountered in six decades.

Booker T. Washington: combined conference and memorial button

1916

On July 4, 1881, a deal between a former slave-owning Alabama politician who wanted black votes and a former slave and community leader who wanted a school for his people resulted in what became Tuskegee University. Thirty adults were in the first class, and Booker T. Washington (1856–1915) was the institution's first principal. From the 1890s until his death at age fifty-nine, Washington was the recognized leader of the African American community. He was famous as an educator, author, and presidential adviser. His appearance as a dinner guest of Theodore Roosevelt at the White House on October 16, 1901, was both groundbreaking and viciously condemned by many. This button commemorates the annual Tuskegee Negro Conference, an event started in 1890 as a venue where rural blacks could discuss their problems and look for solutions. The January 1916 meeting promoted on this button must have been especially somber, as it followed Washington's death the previous November.

Baby Charles Lindbergh Jr.: the murder trial of Bruno Richard Hauptmann

1935

H. L. Mencken, iconic 1930s journalist, satirist, cultural critic, and scholar of American English, called it "the biggest story since the Resurrection." Exaggeration, sure, but in the frenzy of the 1935 trial in the small, rural town of Flemington, New Jersey, not so far from the truth. Eight years earlier, Charles Lindbergh, at age twenty-five, had gone from unknown pilot in the fledgling airmail postal service to being adored as America's greatest hero. His thirty-three and one-half hours in the air, alone and nonstop, from Roosevelt Field on Long Island, New York, to Le Bourget Aerodrome near Paris conferred upon him America's great blessing or curse: celebrity. This eventually made his twenty-month-old son, Charles Jr., a target. A fifty thousand dollar ransom was paid on April 2, 1932, but on May 12, 1932, the remains of the baby were found with his skull crushed along a country road four miles from the Lindbergh estate in Hopewell Township. Serial numbers on the ransom money led to the arrest of Bruno Richard Hauptmann (1899–1936), a German-born carpenter living in New York City. This 2¼-inch photo button suspending a "Press" ribbon was used at the forty-four-day "trial of the century." More than seven hundred reporters and photographers overwhelmed the town. The trial ended on February 14, 1935, with Hauptmann's conviction; his death sentence was carried out on April 3, 1936, after two appeals were rejected by the US Supreme Court.

HOPALONG CASSIDY
DAILY IN THE
CHICAGO TRIBUNE
1950

WOLFMAN JACK
"have mercy, baby!"
XERB 1090
1967

The NEW FRONTIER
MAN of the YEAR
Astronaut John Glenn
1962

3 STOOGES
with
"fuzzie" and Uncle Jim
weat-tv Channel 12
1958

TO THE U.S.A. AND 180 MILLION LOYAL CITIZENS WHO WILL FOLLOW
OUR YOUNG PRESIDENT FORWARD AS HE LEADS US SAFELY THROUGH PERILOUS ATOMIC YEARS
1961

I'm a
OFFICIAL
BEATLES FAN
PAUL McCARTNEY
RINGO "RINGS" STARR
GEORGE HARRISON
JOHN LENNON
© NEMS ENT. LTD. 64
1964

I LUV THOSE ROLLING STONES!!
1966

HANDS OFF
LENNY BRUCE
1964

PEOPLE FOR PLAY
Maurice Sendak
EAST 85TH ST. PLAYGROUND ASS'N., INC.
1961

TRANSCENDENTAL MEDITATION
1967

THE FIRST
HEAD
1967

BELLS & BEADS & ALL YOUR NEEDS
MAMA HIPPIE
1967

HANDS OFF
TIM LEARY
1967

WE WILL BURY YOU

1966

CHARLIE WHITMAN LOVED PUPPIES

1967

JAVITS

1968

DRAFT TWIGGY

1967

AMERICA SALUTES FIRST MEN ON THE MOON

ARMSTRONG COLLINS ALDRIN
APOLLO XI
JULY 1969

1969

GIVE PEACE A CHANCE

WAR IS OVER!

JOHN & YOKO

1969

BUTTON COLLECTORS FOR HUMPHREY MUSKIE

1968

peter max

1968

CAVETT

HAS IT!

1969

ANGELA DAVIS DAY

FREE ANGELA BAIL NOW
CENTRAL PARK ~ SEPTEMBER 25, 1971

1971

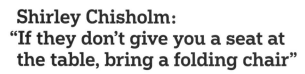

Shirley Chisholm:
"If they don't give you a seat at the table, bring a folding chair"

1972 Shirley Chisholm (1924–2005) was born in Brooklyn to parents recently arrived from the Caribbean. A career in childcare and education led to her interest in politics. Her first campaign, using the slogan "Unbought and Unbossed," earned her a 1968 victory in New York's Twelfth Congressional District, making her the first black woman elected to Congress. Although she represented urban Bedford-Stuyvesant, she was assigned to the House Agricultural Committee. Turning the insult to advantage, she worked with Kansas senator Robert Dole to direct surplus food to an expanded food stamp program. In 1971, she was a founding member of the Congressional Black Caucus as well as the National Women's Political Caucus. In 1972, she became the first black candidate to pursue a major party's nomination for president and the first woman to appear in a US presidential debate. As this 1¼-inch button shows, Chisholm presented herself as a potential "President of All the People." She received 152 votes during the first roll call at the 1972 Democratic convention, coming in fourth to nominee George McGovern's first place. President Barack Obama awarded the Presidential Medal of Freedom posthumously to her in a White House ceremony in November 2015.

JACKSON
5

FAN CLUB

OF
PHILADELPHIA, PA.

1967

1971

LET THERE BE FRIGHT

DR. SHOCK

© 1970

1970

ONLY 25 YEARS OLD
AND THEY'RE DOING
MY LIFE STORY!

1975

1973

I Watch Misteroger's Neighborhood

Channels 67, 73, 28

1973

NEW YORK JAZZ REPERTORY CO.

Louis Armstrong

U.S.S.R. '75

1975

1971

BLACK HISTORY ~ WOMEN'S HISTORY
Fannie Lou Hamer
1917–1977
Women for Racial & Economic Equality

1977

I SAW BETTE AT THE PALACE

1973

1984

DYKES with BIKES

1978

JACQUES COUSTEAU'S LIVING SEA

1974

FREE MARTHA MITCHELL

1973

Christiaan Barnard: a new era for medicine and buttons

1967

On December 3, 1967, the South African cardiac surgeon Christiaan Barnard (1922–2001) performed the world's first successful heart transplant. The donor was Denise Darvall, declared brain-dead after being struck by a car in Cape Town. The recipient was fifty-four-year-old Louis Washkansky, who regained full consciousness before dying of pneumonia eighteen days later. This 1¼-inch button celebrating Dr. Barnard came from Underground Uplift Unlimited, a head shop at 28 St. Marks Place in New York's East Village opened in May 1966 by Randolfe Wicker, a self-described "hippie capitalist" and "multifaceted activist" (see APPENDIX B). Similar stores sprang up across the United States in cities with concentrations of young adults, with Wicker as the primary button distributor. Typical products included rolling papers, pipes, bongs, incense, candles, posters, and a wide variety of cheeky, often drug- or sex-related slogan buttons priced at 25¢ each. The button achieved a new level of popularity, with slogans like Go Both Ways, The Medium Is the Message, and This Button Is Just an Attempt to Communicate.

DRIVE CAREFULLY . . . DR. BARNARD IS WAITING

CRAZY EDDIE® WON'T BE BEAT

1975

BRUCE LEE

1978

A WILD & CRAZY GUY

1978

YOUR 15 MINUTES ARE UP

1987

WOLFMAN JACK'S DISCO PARTY

RIVIERA HOTEL, LAS VEGAS
Oct. 11-17, 1979

1979

FREE NELSON MANDELA

1981

ROCK AGAINST REAGAN

1983-84 ALL POINTS TOUR ★ CALL 212-533-5027

1983

SPRINGSTEEN FOR PRESIDENT 1980

1980

LADY DIANA SPENCER — THE PRINCE OF WALES

29th JULY 1981

1981

1988

BOYCOTT CHIQUITA
1979

STOP POLICE BRUTALITY!
JUSTICE FOR RODNEY KING!
Movement for a Peoples Assembly
(212) 777-1246
1991

FREE ABBIE!
NO MORE POLITICAL PRISONERS
1980

HULKAMANIA™
1988

AMERICA MOURNS IT'S LOSS
Space Shuttle 7-Challenger Heroes
JAN.28,1986
1986

SONNY BONO
U.S. SENATE '92
1992

HOWARD STERN FOR GOVERNOR
92.3FM K-ROCK
1994

© WOMEN'S POLITICAL ALLIANCE 1991 · P.O. BOX 470 STILLWATER, MN 55082 (612) 430-2015
I BELIEVE ANITA HILL
1991

SWAMP THATCHER
1988

SEXUALLY SPEAKING with Dr. Ruth
2012

GILDA'S CLUB
1995

Places

Pin-back buttons began to represent a global perspective in early 1897, when Whitehead & Hoag offered collectors "Flags of Different Nations" at a cost of 5¢ each or $1.20 for all sixty countries. Country, state, city, historical, and even US Weather Service flags were the most popular subjects among the early buttons issued as sets. All the major companies who promoted their products with free buttons issued flag sets, among them Sweet Caporal and High Admiral cigarettes, American Pepsin and Wrigley's Sweet 16 gum, and Earl Confections. A surge in civic pride buttons occurred in 1898, to celebrate a city's founding centennial or to tout an advantageous geographic location ideal for distributing goods via rail networks. Even city disasters resulted in buttons, with two different known examples for the twenty-fifth anniversary in 1896 of the 1871 Chicago fire (see page 78), two for the Baltimore fire of February 7, 1904 (see one of these on page 140), and a real photo button showing the aftermath of buildings destroyed by the San Francisco earthquake of April 18, 1906 (see page 143). Other common subjects included landmarks such as bridges, monuments, beaches, parks, and natural wonders.

ONTARIO BEACH PARK
GRAND OPENING
JUNE 4TH 1906

1906

1910
WHERE LIFE
IS WORTH LIVING
DETROIT

1910

TASHMOO PARK

1905

ATLANTIC CITY
1911

1911

MISS SPOKANE GREETS YOU
1903

INDEPENDENCE HALL, DEDICATED OCT. 26TH, 1898
1898

WYOMING – HOME OF THE BUCKING BRONCHO AND HIS BUSTER
1903

THE GREAT TEXAS STATE FAIR DALLAS SEPT. 28 – OCT. 13 1901.
1901

SOUVENIR OF THE BALTIMORE FIRE.
1904

DERBY DAY SEPT. 13, 1904 TOPEKA, KAN.
1904

COLORADO State Fair PUEBLO SEPT. 26-30-1904.
1904

COLDWATER 1900
1900

ROCKY MOUNTAIN NATIONAL PARK DEDICATION SEPT. 4, 1915

Dedication Day: Rocky Mountain National Park

1915

The US National Park System was inaugurated when Yellowstone National Park opened in 1872; President Woodrow Wilson later established the National Park Service in 1916. Today, there are over four hundred national parks. This 1¼-inch button, made by Colorado Badge, was likely worn by one of the two thousand people in attendance at the opening of Rocky Mountain National Park. Dedication festivities took place in a large open meadow east of the town of Estes Park, with local communities vying to see who could supply the most attendees. Newspapers urged residents to put banners on their "machines" to make it clear what town they represented during the motorized trek from the Majestic Hotel at 7:30 AM for the run to Estes Park. Stephen Mather, assistant to the Secretary of the Interior, donned a raincoat for his speech, but as the program continued, clouds parted and the sun emerged, highlighting the nearby Longs Peak in its coat of new snow. The authors know of only one button to survive this event.

Theodore Roosevelt NATIONAL MEMORIAL PARK
MEDORA, N. DAK.
DEDICATION JUNE 4, 1949

1949

YOU CAN SEE THIS AT BICYCLE TREE SNOHOMISH CITY, WASH.

1913

"THE CORNER STONE OF A NATION"
1620
PLYMOUTH ROCK

1906

CANNON MOUNTAIN TRAMWAY
FRANCONIA NOTCH NEW HAMPSHIRE

1940

OLD MAN OF THE MOUNTAINS
WHITE MTS. N.H.

1938

ONTONAGON CENTENNIAL
1940
ONTONAGON BOULDER

1940

MISSOURI
WE CAN "SHOW YOU"
100,000 STRONG
Robert R. Smith, Director
"SHOW ME"
BUFFALO, 1911.

1911 ACTUAL SIZE

The Long Beach Festival of the Sea: "the most stupendous show ever held in the West; the most magnificent spectacle ever offered"

1908 Enticing advertising for the September 1908 Long Beach Festival of the Sea was matched by this stunning 2⅛-inch button produced by Bastian Brothers. A scallop shell provides the backdrop for a lovely mermaid fussing with her hair as she poses above blue ocean water accompanied by sea snakes forming the lettering. While the button's design appears fanciful, it represents an actual performance at the festival, according to the *Los Angeles Herald*, involving a "delicately colored seashell, rimmed with incandescents and banked with flowers and palms, which rears itself high above the surf," as well as a fairy who "accomplishes the transformation of the 'mermaid queen' into the queen of the Festival of the Sea."

"I Have a Dream":
Dr. King's March on Washington

1963 The hundredth anniversary of President Abraham Lincoln's Emancipation Proclamation was celebrated in 1963. A. Philip Randolph and Bayard Rustin planned a commemorative march in Washington, DC, for August 28. The resulting alliance of civil rights, labor, and religious groups promised to bring a huge crowd to the National Mall. Created as a fundraiser, this official button was produced in two sizes, 2¼ and 3½ inches. By twenty days before the march, forty-two thousand buttons were in circulation and the crowd goal was one hundred thousand. Instead, two hundred fifty thousand people filled the National Mall, from the Lincoln Memorial to the Washington Monument. They became witnesses to Dr. King's historic "I Have a Dream" speech. This enormously successful march has received much credit for the passage of the Civil Rights Act of 1964 and the Voting Rights Act of 1965.

Summer of Love: a victim of its own success

1967 Two early San Francisco leaders, Henry Haight and Munroe Ashbury, are honored by signs at the intersection of Haight and Ashbury Streets. The street signs bearing their names on this 1¼-inch psychedelic, Day-Glo button are emblematic of the 1960s hippie movement. In the 1950s, overflow from San Francisco's North Beach bohemian community had settled in the quaint and less expensive Haight-Ashbury area. In June 1966, an estimated fifteen thousand hippies occupied the large, low-rent Victorian houses. By the following Summer of Love, one hundred thousand had been drawn to the area and overwhelmed it. School openings in September reduced the pressure, but on October 6, 1967, the Diggers street theater group performed a funeral procession complete with a trinket-filled casket to proclaim "the death of the hippie."

UNCLE DON'S PLAYLAND CLUB
Rye, N. Y.
1937

KING·KOLD CARNIVAL
FEB. 2-3-4
GRAND FORKS
1951
NO. DAK.
1951

MARDI GRAS
MARCH, 5th 1935
NEW ORLEANS, LA.
1935

I'm from MASSACHUSETTS
NATIONAL GRANGE WORCESTER, 1941
1941

POPE COUNTY 1953 PAGEANT
MAY 15, 1953
FIRST COURT HOUSE 1866
1953

WILLIAMS POTATO DAY
OCT. 12 1968
15th ANNUAL
WILLIAMS MINN.
802
1968

HEMISFAIR · PLAZA
SAN ANTONIO TEXAS
1968

SHUT DOWN WALL STREET
4-23 1990
1990

the Great Boston Kite Festival
May 17th
Franklin Park
1969

SMOKEY'S TIMBERTENNIAL
AUG. 14,15,16 1964
INTERNATIONAL FALLS, MINN.
PREVENT FOREST FIRES
1964

U.S.A. OUT OF PANAMA
PANAMA
1990

SPRING OF 1983 OPENING!
© 1982 Walt Disney Productions
Tokyo Disneyland
1983

BEAUTIFUL KAUAI
1986

Studio 54
The Big 40
P.B.'s Party
1 • 22 • 78
1978

The slogan that saved NY

1977

In 1977, in an effort to help a bankrupt city, the New York State Department of Commerce commissioned Milton Glaser to design a logo that could promote the city and some sense of unity. Glaser comments: "I ♥ NY was a state-initiated campaign during a period when the city was at its darkest moment. It was more than a slogan; it was a cry from the population in response to a dangerous condition. It did not attempt to persuade; it merely tried to give voice to what we were all feeling at that time. As a result, it had a sense of urgency and authenticity that spread throughout the city, the state, and ultimately the world." Now, it's probably one of the most-used modern images, often copied, and repurposed in many languages. Glaser has explained its enduring graphic appeal: "You have to figure out that the *I* is a complete word, then you have to figure out that the heart is a symbol for an experience, then you have to figure out that *NY* are the initials for a place. We know that the issue in all communication is moving the brain, and puzzles move the brain. This one makes everyone feel good because they solved the problem." This logo has become nearly as iconic as the city itself. It's lasted over forty years unchanged and has generated tens of millions in revenue for the state of New York—and has filled the hearts of residents and tourists alike.

Pop Shop: art for everyone

1986

Keith Haring's subway drawings and street graffiti spread worldwide in the early 1980s. In April 1986, he opened Pop Shop at 292 Lafayette Street in New York's SoHo neighborhood. The retail store was covered in his floor-to-ceiling murals and offered posters, T-shirts, and, of course, buttons (most are, like this logo button, 1 inch). Haring stated, "I wanted to continue the same sort of communication as with the subway drawings. I wanted to attract the same wide range of people and I wanted a place where, yes, not only collectors could come, but also kids from the Bronx.... This was still an art statement." In 1990, at age thirty-one, Haring died of AIDS-related complications.

SOUVENIR OF NEW YORK CITY
UNITED NATIONS

1958

Save SoHo

1979

"I've been to the Top of the World"

The Observation Deck
at the World Trade Center

1975

L.A.-NO WAY!

KEEP DAVE IN
NEW YORK!

1992

Sports

Over the past 125 years, the three most popular sports in the United States—baseball, football, and basketball—have inspired the greatest number of buttons, but the interests of the early adopters of pin-back buttons were much different. The button's invention coincided with the bicycle craze of the 1890s, specifically the boom year of 1896, when hundreds of bicycle manufacturers were ready to advertise their brand of wheel with giveaway buttons. Bicycle racing in recently built velodromes became an exciting new sport, from short sprints to monster marathons lasting up to six days. Indeed, bicycle racing was so popular that there were six events at the first modern Olympic Games in 1896, attracting fifteen contestants from five nations. ● Boxing promoters and freelancing vendors also quickly embraced the button. Most notably, the 1897 St. Patrick's Day contest in Carson City, Nevada, between James J. Corbett and Bob Fitzsimmons produced at least ten different buttons picturing one or the other or both. The first boxing buttons to be included in a set of advertising giveaways also appeared in 1897, courtesy of Cameo Pepsin gum. ● In 1897, when Whitehead & Hoag published a catalog titled "Good News for Button Collectors," two of the fourteen series on offer depicted past winners of 1880s and '90s America's Cup yacht races, and a small series titled "Athletes" comprised seven bicycle racers, three boxers, two sculling champions, one wrestler, and one strongman, Eugen Sandow. Over the years, nearly every sport has been represented by at least a few buttons. Among the earliest with known years of issue are baseball (1896), fishing (1896), horse racing (1898), football (1898), basketball (1903), the Olympics (1906), power boating (1908), and bowling (1909). Together, sports buttons provide mementos of our favorite teams and athletes, reminding us of legendary names from long ago.

Football buttons: early twentieth-century macho diversions

1898

The earliest football button the authors have encountered is from 1898. It shows a fierce, spike-collar-wearing bulldog with giant canines shredding an Auburn University pennant with surrounding slogan "'EAT 'EM UP' GA." This is followed by a few more college game buttons, one from the Yale-Princeton 1921 matchup in New Haven and another for a Grange member's 1922 trip to the Polo Grounds to see Syracuse take on Penn State. The earliest individual player button is a 1¼-inch real photo of Harold Edward "Red" Grange (1903–1991), ca. 1929. Nicknamed "The Galloping Ghost," he played eight seasons bewteen 1925 to 1934—first for the Chicago Bears, then the football New York Yankees, then back to the Bears in 1929. His NFL career was fumble-less. While a few individual player buttons followed Grange, the vast majority of professional team–related buttons carry a team name or, starting in 1967, name the teams playing in the Super Bowl. In addition, a wide variety of high school and college buttons were issued for annual homecoming games, mainly during the 1930s through the '60s. These were often done in a humorous cartoon style, with one school mascot besting the other.

Bicycle racing:
superstars on two wheels

1901

The newly introduced safety bicycle with tires of equal size initiated the bicycle craze of the 1890s and revolutionized bicycle racing. Professional riders competing on a banked wooden track in velodromes became a nationwide sensation, with the best riders accorded superstar status. The world's first African American sports superstar was Marshall Walter "Major" Taylor (1878–1932). Born in Indianapolis, he was led to racing through his work in bicycle shops. As a teenager, he moved to Worcester, Massachusetts, where his 1894 amateur team was the See Saw Cycling Club. He went pro in 1896 and by 1899 was the world cycling champion. The next year, he was US sprint champion, living up to his nickname, the "Worcester Whirlwind." Taylor's first button appearances came in 1898. On one issued by a Waltham, Massachusetts, bicycle seller, he endorses Orient Cycles, and on the other he is shown with competitor Eddie McDuffie under the title "Black vs White" (see page 150), promoting a Boston race with a $1,500 purse. The firearms and bicycle manufacturing company Iver Johnson sponsored Taylor in 1900 on the race circuit and in 1901 put him on this ⅞-inch button, making these three buttons the first to picture an African American sports star endorsing an event and consumer products.

BOWLING TOURNAMENT 1942

1942

JIM THORPE: FORMER CARLISLE ATHLETE
CARLISLE, PA. - JUNE 13-14-15, 1933

1933

Imp'd O. R. M.

I'm for WILLKIE
JOE LOUIS

1940

MISS CAPITOL CLASSIC
1946 CAPITOL CLASSIC

1946

XIth OLYMPIC GAMES
LOS ANGELES 1932

1932

'44
DUCKS
Unlimited

1944

JOLLY ROLLING BUDDIES

1942

CHICAGO
WHITE SOX

1958

COLTS VS GIANTS
NFL 1959
WORLD CHAMPIONSHIP

1959

GINO MARCHETTI DAY
DEC. 13
BOOSTER
1964
BILL PELLINGTON DAY

1964

JOE DiMAGGIO CLUB
BUITONI
FOODS CORP.

1949

"MR. MET"

1966

DUNCAN YO-YO TOURNEY
No. 77
CONTESTANT

1948

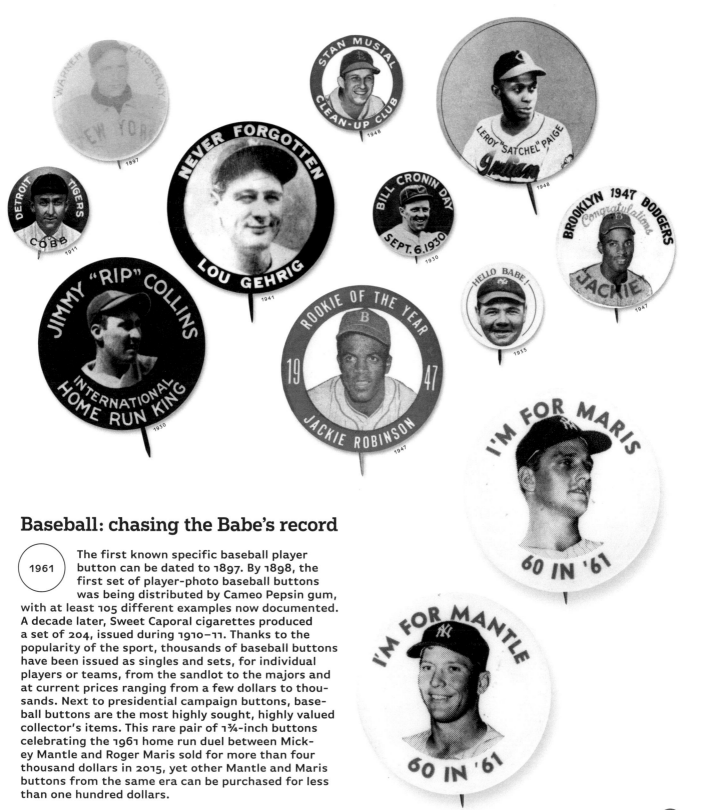

WARNER CATORN.Y NEW YORK 1897

STAN MUSIAL CLEAN-UP CLUB 1948

LEROY "SATCHEL" PAIGE Indians 1948

DETROIT TIGERS COBB 1911

NEVER FORGOTTEN LOU GEHRIG 1941

BILL CRONIN DAY SEPT. 6 1930 1930

BROOKLYN 1947 BODGERS Congratulations JACKIE 1947

JIMMY "RIP" COLLINS INTERNATIONAL HOME RUN KING 1930

ROOKIE OF THE YEAR 19 47 JACKIE ROBINSON 1947

HELLO BABE! 1935

I'M FOR MARIS 60 IN '61

I'M FOR MANTLE 60 IN '61

Baseball: chasing the Babe's record

1961

The first known specific baseball player button can be dated to 1897. By 1898, the first set of player-photo baseball buttons was being distributed by Cameo Pepsin gum, with at least 105 different examples now documented. A decade later, Sweet Caporal cigarettes produced a set of 204, issued during 1910–11. Thanks to the popularity of the sport, thousands of baseball buttons have been issued as singles and sets, for individual players or teams, from the sandlot to the majors and at current prices ranging from a few dollars to thousands. Next to presidential campaign buttons, baseball buttons are the most highly sought, highly valued collector's items. This rare pair of 1¾-inch buttons celebrating the 1961 home run duel between Mickey Mantle and Roger Maris sold for more than four thousand dollars in 2015, yet other Mantle and Maris buttons from the same era can be purchased for less than one hundred dollars.

ROPER SNOW SUITS FOR BOYS AND GIRLS

1910

LACONIA SLED DOG DERBY
WORLD'S CHAMPIONSHIP
FEB. 7, 8, 9, 1936

1936

Northville, N.Y.
'40 '41
Winter Sports

1940

I'm Boosting
The CADILLAC WINTER SPORTS CLUB 1939

1939

SOUVENIR OF WINTER OLYMPICS 1960 SQUAW VALLEY

1960

"CHING" JOHNSON
ARCO SKATE
SKATING CLUB MEMBER

1933

Golf: an elite sport goes public

1907 & 1960

Although it cannot be proved, it seems the first golf button is a humble 1¼-inch model reading "Pinehurst 1907." That was the year Pinehurst No. 2 opened at the North Carolina resort of the same name. Designed by the renowned Donald Ross, this course remains among the world's most celebrated. For decades after 1907, there is nary a golf button in sight, with the exception of a single 1930 rarity picturing and naming Bobby Jones, a famous golfer of that era (see page 153). Golf buttons began to slowly proliferate around 1960, the date of this 1¾-inch portrait of Arnold Palmer (1929–2016) that commands "Join Arnie's Army." Palmer won the US Open that year and enjoyed a career spanning six decades and sixty-two PGA tour titles, during which time the popularity of playing golf and watching it on television took off. Palmer is credited with democratizing golf, transforming the once-elite pastime to one accessible to all. Although very few other buttons featuring professional players appear to have been made, there have been many buttons related to golf tournaments as well as a small pool of mostly 1930s-era caddy-identification buttons with serial numbers, made during those days when golf was an elite pursuit.

Horse racing: the equal-opportunity sport

1900

The vast majority of horse racing buttons from the twentieth century are related to thoroughbred horses or horse races, for example, Secretariat's 1973 victories and the annual Kentucky Derby buttons. The earliest go back to around 1900, when High Admiral cigarettes created a set of twenty giveaway buttons showing famous jockeys wearing their colors. At the same time, American Pepsin gum and Little Jockey cigarettes issued a set of nine (see page 152 for one example). Horse racing was one of the few professional sports that allowed African American and female jockeys. Among these twenty-nine buttons are at least three black jockeys and five women jockeys. A distinctly small but popular subset of horse racing buttons are those related to harness racing. The standouts among these, both 1½ inches, are one design in black and red and one in full color, both for the most famous trotter of all: Dan Patch (1896–1916). Like bicycle racing, harness racing was immensely popular in the early twentieth century. Dan Patch broke the speed record for various track distances around fourteen times in the early 1900s. He was the first animal celebrity product endorser of the twentieth century; while his fame was used to hawk everything from whiskey to sheet music, his endorsement of International Stock Food was likely nearest and dearest to his own heart.

1965

1950

1973

1951

1989

RIGGS POWER

ON YOUR LOCAL ABC-TV STATION•THURS..SEPT.20

1973

RECORDAMOS A CLEMENTE

WE REMEMBER CLEMENTE

1972

KING POWER

ON YOUR LOCAL ABC-TV STATION•THURS..SEPT.20

1973

OPENING DAY II 1986

"A Little Respect"

Mets

1986

ANGEL CITY DERBY GIRLS

2012

1971 FAREWELL 1987

Dr. J!

1987

Boxing: "I am the greatest"

1975

Buttons amply document a century of championship fights, at least those of heavyweights. There are multiple buttons for the 1897 match between Jim Corbett and Bob Fitzsimmons. Also commemorated are Jack Johnson vs. James Jeffries in 1910, Jack Dempsey vs. Tommy Gibbons in 1923, Dempsey vs. Gene Tunney in 1926, Joe Louis in the 1930s, and Floyd Patterson in the 1950s and '60s. Particularly well covered are the years of Muhammad Ali, who was born Cassius Marcellus Clay Jr. (1942–2016), beginning with his 1964 victory over Sonny Liston. Ali beat twenty-one boxers for the world heavyweight title in famous matches that included the 1974 Rumble in the Jungle (against George Foreman, with one billion television viewers worldwide) and the 1975 Thrilla in Manila (against Joe Frazier). This 2⅛-inch button was likely used as a bookseller's trade show promo for the 1975 softcover *The Holy Warrior: An Illustrated Biography* by Don Atyeo and Felix Dennis.

Transportation

Soon after the button's 1896 debut, every existing mode of transportation was being colorfully portrayed and vying for attention on hats, jackets, and shirts. Vehicle makers drove button production with their advertising. Foremost were bicycle manufacturers, followed by producers of the dominant family vehicle types: the buggy, the carriage, and the farm wagon. ● In 1898, the first automobile button appeared, picturing two fashionably dressed married couples in the front and rear seats of their open-air Montgomery Ward Electric Horseless Carriage (see page 162). Thereafter, buttons for car brands, car shows, races, and products such as gasoline, oil, and tires grew to dominate the transportation category. ● In aviation, a button was produced for the 1905 appearance of a piloted airship at a Brockton, Massachusetts, fair (see page 165). The Wright Brothers appear on a 1909 Dayton, Ohio, button to celebrate their powered flight and homecoming (see page 165), and the first dated button to show an airplane was issued for a 1910 aviation contest in Los Angeles (see page 166). Lindbergh's celebrated solo transatlantic flight of 1927 and his subsequent tour of ninety-two cities in all forty-eight states made him the most frequently seen person on a button (other than presidential candidates) up to that time (see page 170). The Space Age arrived with a button commemorating the 1961 suborbital flight of "America's First Astronaut Navy Lt. Comdr. Alan B. Shepard" (see page 171). The next year, about a half dozen buttons marked the successful three-orbit flight of John Glenn on February 20, 1962. As President John F. Kennedy's 1961 pledge to put a man on the moon was realized on July 20, 1969, button makers responded with an estimated fifty different designs (see page 171).

THE CUNARD · WHITE STAR, LTD.
SUPER-LINER
QUEEN MARY

PARAGON S. S. AGENCY
1843 PURCHASE ST.
NEW BEDFORD,
MASS.

1936

0000

C.M. ST. P. & P.R.R.
25
V.E.A.

1946

FLY TO

DAYTON

1937

THE CAR OF CARS

FORD V·8
FOR 1935

1935

GOOD YEAR

1937

MINNEAPOLIS AUTO SHOW
MAR. 2–9, '07.

1907

HENRY H. VAN BRUNT. VEHICLES. BEST ON THE GLOBE.

1910

TRIP TO FRISCO CONTEST

CONTEST ENDS JUNE 17, 1915.

FRISCO

DAYTON

THE THOMAS MFG. CO. DAYTON, O.

COLON

PANAMA

1915

The electric horseless carriage: the automobile's first button

1898

The first known button to feature an automobile shows off a machine created by the American Electric Vehicle Company in Chicago. Beating Richard Sears to the mail order business by over twenty years, Aaron Montgomery Ward named it the Montgomery Ward Co. Electric Horseless Carriage. Although this was the only American car to win a gold medal at the 1900 Paris Exposition, electric vehicles were soon surpassed by gasoline vehicles, thanks to the electric starter, quicker refueling, greater mileage range, and a rapidly expanding petroleum infrastructure. A complete collection of car buttons would exceed one thousand different specimens.

Bicycle buttons:
cyclists demand "Good Roads"

1896

The earliest bicycles appeared around 1820. By the 1860s people were riding high-wheels, or velocipedes, and by 1896, the coaster brake and pneumatic tires brought the chain-driven bicycle to the masses. The League of American Wheelmen, promoted on this 1¼-inch button issued in 1896, was the dominant cyclists' group. Founded in Newport, Rhode Island, on May 30, 1880, they advocated for "Good Roads" and devised the rules that governed that era's immensely popular bicycle races. The safety bicycle was selling like hot-cakes in 1896, and hundreds of manufacturers used the just-invented pin-back button and still-novel celluloid-covered lapel stud as major advertising tools. Advertisers greatly favored the lapel stud—possibly due to safety concerns about riding a bike while wearing a device with a protruding pin. By 1898, the League had 103,000 members, but the popularity of the bicycle plummeted in the early twentieth century, and relatively few bicycle buttons were produced thereafter.

STRAP HANGERS LEAGUE
"TWO CENTS IS ENOUGH FOR THIS."
1902

I
Love a Horse
and Carriage
but
OH YOU
TAXICAB
1905

CHECKER CAB
UNION
· INDEPENDENT ·
J. J. KULK
2003 W. CHAMBERS ST.
36
1921

WE·WANT·A·BROAD·ST·SUBWAY
PHILA. & SUBURBAN
ELEVATED R.R.
TO FRANKFORD 20 MIN.
TO WAYNE JUNCTION 14 MIN.
TO STRAWBERRY MANSION
13 MIN.
1926

Ship and boat buttons: wearing the waterways

1910 Nautical buttons cover many subcategories and were quite popular with early button collectors. In the late 1890s, Whitehead & Hoag issued button sets of Spanish-American War military vessels, sailboat winners of the America's Cup, and ocean liners. Other subjects include Great Lakes steamers, river paddle wheelers, ferries, motorboats, yacht clubs, and hydroplane boat races. The most notorious ship to be featured on buttons (second only to the RMS *Queen Mary*) was the RMS *Lusitania*, also part of what was then the Cunard–White Star Line. At her 1906 launch, she became the world's largest passenger ship, but she carried the title only three months before losing it to her sister ship, the RMS *Mauretania*. Today, the *Lusitania* is better known as a casualty of World War I. On May 7, 1915, the ship was off the Irish coast, near the end of its 202nd Atlantic crossing, when tragedy struck: a German submarine put a torpedo into her starboard bow. Moments later, a second explosion caused by munitions she was secretly carrying sealed her fate. There were 1,198 deaths, including 128 Americans who had ignored Imperial German Embassy warnings placed in fifty US newspapers that those traveling in the war zone of British waters did so "at their own risk." This 1-inch button from around 1910 specifies "Hold Baggage," and its mate specifies "Hand Baggage."

Railroad, subway, and trolley buttons: getting from here to there

(1934) Illustrated on a 1¼-inch Whitehead & Hoag button from 1896 is an aerial view of the winding train track that forms "The Loop Near Georgetown, Colo." This narrow-gauge railroad, deemed an engineering marvel, was completed in 1884 to connect the mining towns of Georgetown and Silver Plume, Colorado (see page 165). A huge variety of rail-related buttons followed over the next sixty years. The most common are monthly union dues buttons for various occupations, along with a few featuring protective gear such as gloves and overalls, a good number advocating rail crossing safety ("Death Is So Permanent! / Drive Carefully!"; see page 166), some commemorative examples (mostly related to early twentieth-century New York City subways and bridges), and promotional buttons for the many passenger and freight lines across the country. One of the most striking is a 1¼-inch blue and silver art deco beauty for the Pioneer Zephyr, America's first diesel streamline train, looking like something out of *Buck Rogers in the 25th Century*. On May 26, 1934, the train set a famous dawn-to-dusk speed record, traveling from Denver to Chicago nonstop at an average speed near 78 mph and a top speed of 112½ mph. The run was the basis for the train's nickname, the "Silver Streak," and the 1976 movie of the same name starring Gene Wilder, Jill Clayburgh, and Richard Pryor. Retired in 1960, the Zephyr can still be seen in Chicago's Museum of Science and Industry.

Aviation buttons:
Lindbergh astounds the world

1927

Buttons have documented countless aviation events, most commonly air shows, air races, and record-breaking flights. The biggest record breaker of the twentieth century was in 1927: the solo, nonstop, transatlantic New York–Paris flight of Charles Lindbergh. The celebrity accorded Lindbergh was unprecedented. From July 20 to October 23 of that year, Lindbergh, flying the Spirit of St. Louis, visited 92 cities in 48 states and gave 147 speeches. The number of Lindbergh button designs issued in 1927 approaches one hundred, a staggering number exceeded only by some presidential candidates. Lindbergh's remarkable year ended with the American toy manufacturer Louis Marx and Company issuing one of the rarest of all Lindbergh-related buttons, a 1¼-inch specimen proclaiming "Marx for Toys," with Santa piloting a Lindy-style plane inscribed "Spirit of 1927."

APOLLO 11 ASTRONAUTS

Neil A. Armstrong
Commander

Michael Collins
Command-Module Pilot

Edwin E. Aldrin, Jr.
Lunar-Module Pilot

SUNDAY JULY 20th 1969 — FIRST MAN ON THE MOON

NEIL A. ARMSTRONG

FIRST MEN ON THE MOON

1969

AROUND THE WORLD IN 80 MINUTES

1st AMERICAN IN ORBIT

ASTRONAUT JOHN GLENN

WELCOME BACK TO EARTH

1962

Space flight buttons: "...built by the lowest bidder"

1961

The idea of human travel to other worlds (and extraterrestrial travel to our world) goes back centuries. During the twentieth century, as various forms of mass media developed, space travel was the subject of science fiction novels, movies, pulp magazines, radio broadcasts, comics, television shows, and video games. In 1961, this realm shifted from fiction to reality on April 12, when Soviet cosmonaut Yuri Gagarin (1934–1968) became the first person in space. That same year, on May 5, Alan Shepard (1923–1998) became America's first man to reach space as part of a suborbital flight. Reporters later queried Shepard about his thoughts as he sat at the tip of a Redstone rocket awaiting launch. His reply: "The fact that every part of this ship was built by the lowest bidder."

AMERICA'S FIRST ASTRONAUT

NAVY LT. COMDR. ALAN B. SHEPARD

War & Anti-war

War buttons spike on the home front in response to specific military actions, especially if shots are fired. The United States' first war after the pin-back button's invention was the Spanish-American War of 1898. Although the war lasted only from April 21 to August 13, more than seventy-five designs were produced. ● Fortuitously for button buyers (but not Whitehead & Hoag, the celluloid button maker), the invention of lithographed metal buttons by J. L. Lynch of Chicago coincided with President Woodrow Wilson's announcement on April 2, 1917, that the United States was entering World War I. Over the next two years, Lynch produced millions upon millions of "decorated metal buttons" for various Liberty Loan and War Savings drives, along with similar quantities for the Red Cross and Salvation Army. Lynch proclaimed the new button technology so revolutionary that it rendered celluloid buttons obsolete; metal buttons were cheaper and faster to manufacture since they didn't require celluloid, paper, or a collet. ● Into the 1920s, many buttons were made as souvenirs of the annual reunions of Civil War veterans, both the Grand Army of the Republic and United Confederate Veterans. By the time of World War II, the button as a communication tool was so valued that button manufacturers were allowed to continue production despite government restrictions on the use of chemicals and metals that applied to most of society. ● While propaganda, patriotism, and fundraising fueled button production during those wars, the button's role in the next major US conflict was much different. President Lyndon Johnson's dramatic escalation of the Vietnam War in 1965 was initially supported by public opinion, but year after year, opposition to the war grew. Between 1965 and 1973, just a few rah-rah America pro–Vietnam War buttons were made. The vast majority of buttons were anti-war, issued to promote strikes, demonstrations, and marches, and to support those jailed for civil disobedience (see "Campaigns & Causes"). ● America's most recent and current engagements around the world have inspired few buttons, with minor exceptions for the Gulf War (1990–91) and the Iraq War (2003–11).

V-J DAY

1945

V
...-

1944

UNCLE SAM CAN COUNT ON ME

1943

WE'LL DO IT!

1942

WOMEN MARCH TO VICTORY

1943

The Civil War: four years of war, decades of reunions

1899 & 1900 The American Civil War was declared "virtually" ended on May 9, 1865 by President Andrew Johnson. By the next year, Union veterans had formed the fraternal organization the Grand Army of the Republic (GAR), which peaked in membership at around 410,000 in 1890. The Southern veterans had local groups but didn't form the national United Confederate Veterans (UCV) until 1889. Their membership peaked at 160,000 around 1899, the year of this 1¾-inch memorial button showing Varina Anne Davis (1864–1898). Widely known as the Daughter of the Confederacy, Miss Winnie Davis was the daughter of Confederacy president Jefferson Davis. In the 1880s, she increasingly became her father's representative at public appearances, making speeches at UCV conventions. She died at age thirty-four, and this button was used to mark her passing at the 1899 UCV convention in Charleston, South Carolina. UCV buttons in general are much scarcer and more valuable than GAR buttons. This 1¾-inch button from the GAR Chicago convention of 1900, showing the earliest button image of what became in the 1950s *MAD* magazine's "What, Me Worry?" boy, is an exception; the only known example sold at auction in 2007 for over eight hundred dollars.

ON GUARD IN THE "SUNNY SOUTH"

1898

1917

MUSTERED OUT.

1898

THIRTEENTH ANNUAL REUNION EX-CONFEDERATE VETERANS HOCONA, TEXAS.

AUG. 14-15-16 1901

1901

DISCHARGED

NO MAS MANILA

1902

GET BEHIND THE GOVERNMENT LIBERTY LOAN OF 1917

1917

LEAGUE TO ENFORCE PEACE

DELEGATE

1919

NATIONAL CONGRESS (IN NINE SECTIONS) FOR A LEAGUE OF NATIONS FEBRUARY 1919

SAVE "OLD IRONSIDES"

1797 1925

1925

LEST WE FORGET GALLIPOLI APRIL 25TH 1915

1915

TO DER KAISER

1915

WHAT WE HAVE WE HOLD

1914

THROUGH THE METROPOLITAN LIFE INSURANCE CO.

I BOUGHT W.S.S. VALUE OF $50

1918

HELP FINLAND

1939

ANTI-CANDY-LEAGUE ARE YOU? M.T.H.S.

1917

OFFICIAL WORKER No 4784 $6,000,000 ARMENIAN & SYRIAN RELIEF

1919

SOUVENIR OF OUR BOYS IN BLUE PACIFIC COAST

1908

CUBA USA MAY-1-98 MAINE

REMEMBERED THE MAINE

1898

The Spanish-American War —and Cuba, too!

1898

The pin-back button was only two years old when war with Spain was declared by President William McKinley in 1898, after the sinking of the battleship USS *Maine* in the harbor of Havana, Cuba. In the brief hostilities, two events stand out. One was Admiral George Dewey's naval victory over the Spanish fleet in the Philippines at the Battle of Manila Bay; thus, many buttons picture Dewey, sometimes with his flagship *Olympia*. A greater number focus on Cuba, where Theodore Roosevelt led his Rough Riders into the Battle of San Juan Hill on July 1, 1898. Related buttons depict US military leaders, the *Maine*, and other US warships, released in sets. Quite a few feature cartoon graphics; the most gruesome of these is this 1¼-inch example showing Uncle Sam using a nail-studded paddle labeled "U.S." to pound bloody holes into a Spaniard's backside, captioned "S-PAIN," accompanied by the title "The Yanko Spanko War."

The buttons depicted include:

- G.A.R. CHAUTAUQUA, JULY 17, 1909 — GENERAL CUSTER (1909)
- THE YANKEE PIG. OH I DON'T KNOW? CUBA (1898)
- BOERS SYMPATHY (1898)
- A WELCOME AWAITS YOU AT ROCHESTER — THE FLOWER CITY 1911 (1911)
- "LAFAYETTE WE COME!" PERSHING-1917 (1917)
- THERE'S A HUNDRED MILLION MORE LIKE ME (1917)
- MY COUNTRY CALLS — JUNE 5TH 1917 (1917)
- MARNE 1914 1918 (1918)
- "HAVE REGISTERED" "CALL TO THE COLORS" COLUMBUS, OHIO·JUNE 5·1917 READY TO DO MY PART (1917)
- ARMENIAN RELIEF (1915)
- ARMISTICE DAY NOV. 11, '20 DANCE PALACE San Diego (1920)

World War I: buttons fund a war

(1917) In 1916, President Woodrow Wilson ran successfully for reelection on a "peace and preparedness" campaign, but nonetheless, war on Germany was declared by Congress on April 6, 1917. During the twenty months that the United States participated in World War I, the government strove to finance the war effort by conducting the greatest-ever PR campaign, asking citizens to buy bonds and War Savings stamps and to contribute to their local "war chest." The button was an integral part as a sign of participation and patriotism. The motto of J. L. Lynch, the inventor of these metal buttons, was "Buttons That Mold Public Opinion." Other popular World War I examples focused on leaders such as General John Pershing; a handful were anti–German Kaiser, and some, like this 1¾-inch button, called for home front patriotism or overseas humanitarian relief. "We're Behind the Man Behind the Gun" also was issued with a white background and blue rim; the yellow version was made in the 1½-inch size as well, but it is rare, with only one known.

WE'RE BEHIND THE MAN BEHIND THE GUN

BUTTON
YOUR
LIP
FOR
DEFENSE

1942

SEALED LIPS
SAVE SHIPS

1943

5th
COLUMN

1942

WHEN
IN DOUBT
SHUT
UP

1943

Buttons pictured with dates:

- WHIP WASTE and WIN! — 1942
- KILL the RATS! MUSSO ADOLPH TOGO — 1942
- THE HERO OF PEARL HARBOR — DORIE MILLER — 1942
- I'M CHINESE FOR U.S.A. 1st - LAST & ALWAYS — 1944
- HIT-'EM-HARD MacARTHUR — 1944
- REGISTERED FOR 1940 NATIONAL DEFENSE — 1940
- THUMBS UP! WE'RE GOING TO WIN WITH OUR CHURCHILL GUTS AND GRIN — THERE'LL ALWAYS BE AN ENGLAND — 1944
- FOR FREEDOM'S SAKE WE'LL CRUSH THE SNAKE BUY BONDS & STAMPS — TOJO — 1943
- NORWAY LIBERATED — 1945
- EXTERMINATE THESE 3 RATS — MUSSI ADOLF TOGO — 1942
- I'M BUYING BONDS FOR BOMBERS 1943 ILLINOIS RURAL YOUTH — 1943
- We'll feed 'em — 1943
- GENERAL GEORGE S. PATTON JR. — 1944
- BLOOD FOR KOREA I HAVE PLEDGED — 1950
- (soldier and woman photo) — 1942

DEFEND YOUR COUNTRY — ©1940 T.B.W.

World War II: Uncle Sam's call to arms

1940 This colorful 1¼-inch button reproduces a close-up image taken from the May 28, 1940, release of a World War II US Army recruiting poster designed by Major Tom B. Woodburn, whose initials appear with a tiny copyright symbol on the button. The poster art appeared on sheet music, 11,300 Railway Express Agency trucks, and this button. One version has a back paper from New York button maker Emress Novelty Co., and another's back paper names Berry Pink Sales Promotions. Berry Pink was a New Jersey man who came up with the idea of recycling glass into marbles. In 1940, he sponsored marble tournaments for children under the age of fifteen across the United States and in Hawaii; likely, this button served as a giveaway to participants. It stands as the single known example of a full-color- process button related to World War II; all other known buttons are printed in spot colors, using mostly red, white, and blue.

Vietnam War:
buttons mobilize the youth

1964–67 On May 2, 1964, the first major student protest against the Vietnam War saw one thousand students marching through New York, from Times Square to the United Nations. The 1¼-inch button at right was produced for that first event, known as the May Second Movement. About a year later, the Students for a Democratic Society held the March on Washington to End the War in Vietnam. The 1½-inch button below was worn at that April 17, 1965, protest, which drew an estimated crowd of twenty thousand—the largest peace protest in US history to that point. As the anti-war and civil rights movements joined forces, hundreds of button designs were created across the United States for the many protests that occurred over the next decade.

Gulf War: yellow ribbon revival

1991 Unlike in the Vietnam War, where 99 percent of the buttons produced were anti-war, in the Gulf War, encompassing Operation Desert Shield and Operation Desert Storm, 99 percent of the buttons supported the war and troops.

Whitehead & Hoag Co.: A Brief History, Including the Invention of the Pin-Back Button

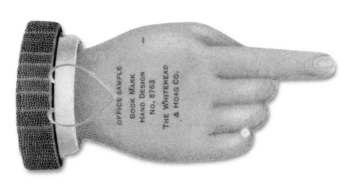 

After the Civil War, the pace of urbanization and industrialization quickened in the eastern United States while settlement of the vast western lands accelerated as the wagon train and, later, the transcontinental railroad came into use. By 1890, during what Mark Twain described as the Gilded Age, the United States' population exceeded sixty million, roughly one-fifth of today's total. US industrial production and per capita income exceeded that of all other nations. However, not all was rosy: the Panic of 1893 set off a depression that affected business owners, workers, and farmers nationwide. This downturn framed the backdrop to the bitterly contested presidential election of 1896, pitting Democratic nominee William Jennings Bryan against the Republican nominee, William McKinley.

At this auspicious moment, a Newark, New Jersey, advertising specialty manufacturer invented the pin-back button in the form that has survived for more than a century. With incredible efficiency, Whitehead & Hoag Co. introduced the pin-back nationwide in 1896 and quickly achieved the capacity to produce one million buttons per day. Button fever swept the nation and created a legion of first-generation button collectors.

The Men

Benjamin S. Whitehead was born in Newark, New Jersey, on January 24, 1858, the son of Edmond B. and Elizabeth Whitehead. His family's roots in the United States predated the Revolution. His father was a deputy collector in the Internal Revenue Service under Presidents Lincoln, Grant, and Garfield. By age twelve, Whitehead had decided to become a printer

and spent time in Newark schools, the Cooper Union in New York City, and the New Jersey Business College. By age fifteen, he ran a modest printing business and achieved early success with an exhibition of his printing samples at the 1876 Centennial Exhibition in Philadelphia, apparently produced on a steam press in his parents' home on Arlington Street.

Whitehead's first listing as a printer appeared in the 1878–79 Newark Directory. In 1882, Whitehead married Fanny M. Thompson, and they had one son, Ray, and one daughter, Helen. Around this time, Whitehead moved his business from his parents' home and opened a new print shop with Benjamin Clark at 96 Market Street in Newark under the name Whitehead and Clark. By 1888, their directory entry read "book, job printer's [sic], badgemakers," and the business had moved to 167 Halsey Street. *Badgemaking* referred to printing inscriptions on silk ribbons to be worn by means of a pin or stickpin; these decorations were popular with political candidates, volunteer fire departments, and fraternal lodges.

Whitehead was a Republican. His personal interests were wide, and his participation in public affairs extensive. He was a trustee of the Centenary Methodist Church and a member, president, or trustee of many other clubs, organizations, and businesses. Still, he found time to travel throughout the United States and to twenty-two other countries, all the while taking photos and recording ideas about novelties that his plant could produce. Whitehead enjoyed music, but his primary hobby was fishing. He collected more than two thousand rods and reels and spent his summers developing an estate on Whitehead's Island, Maine, and at Kezar Lake near Lovell, Maine. In 1903, twelve advertising specialty firms decided to form an industry trade association named the National Association of Advertising Novelty Manufacturers, with Whitehead as the first president. The group continues today as Promotional Products Association International. Benjamin S. Whitehead died at age eighty-two on April 16, 1940.

Chester R. Hoag was born November 28, 1860, in Wellsboro, Pennsylvania. His formal education ended with grammar school, but he was a voracious reader. Hoag arrived in Newark in 1882 looking for work. Soon he was traversing Essex County on a high-wheel bicycle, selling paper and twine for a distributor who paid him eight dollars per week. Hoag made his first appearance in the Newark Directory with a partner, Charles Harrison, in 1886, listed as Harrison & Hoag, suppliers of paper and twine.

Coincidentally, the firm of Harrison & Hoag was just a few doors down the street from Whitehead and Clark, and it appears that this is how Whitehead and Hoag first met and became friends. By 1892, talk of a partnership became reality, and on March 8, the Whitehead & Hoag Co. was incorporated, with fifty thousand dollars authorized in capital stock. Charles Harrison continued in the paper and twine business, but Newark Directory listings for Benjamin Clark cease.

Hoag married Clara L. Osborne, a descendant of a Newark founding family, in 1896. He was very active in establishing the vocational school system in Essex County, was an elder in the Presbyterian Church, and served as a president of the Newark Museum, where he produced a 1928 exhibition *Medals Made in Newark*. The museum still holds many medals made by W&H and donated by Hoag. Like his partner, Hoag loved the outdoors, particularly shooting and fishing, and he traveled the states and abroad to enjoy his hobbies. He had a summer home at Clayton, New York, where he kept several speedboats. After a long illness, Hoag died of a heart ailment on February 28, 1935. Hoag and his wife had a daughter and four sons, with one son, Philip, serving as company president until he died in 1953.

The Company

W&H's first business location in 1892 was in a third-floor loft at 167 Market Street, Newark. They soon moved to 163 Washington Street and expanded further to 161 Washington Street, with additional space on the intersecting Warren Street. Their chief product from 1892 to 1893 was the ribbon badge, but their 1894 Newark Directory ad included a reference to "celluloid badges." These were not yet pin-back buttons but lapel studs consisting of a thin, clear celluloid sheet over a printed paper held in a ¾-inch-diameter silvered metal circular frame with a

slightly extending smaller circle of metal on the reverse, meant to be inserted into a jacket or shirt button hole.

After spending two decades constantly acquiring additional office and manufacturing space at their Washington and Warren Street locations, in March 1910 W&H announced plans to move the business from the city center to the city outskirts by purchasing a large land tract, formerly used as circus grounds, at the intersection of Sussex Avenue and First Street. In 1913, W&H moved into a new five-floor, 125,000-square-foot concrete building with a frontage of 260 feet on Sussex Street and 475 feet on First Street. This factory was a complete printing and lithography plant, with over fifty modern presses, a large art and photo engraving plant in which sketches and plates were made, a button making plant with a capacity exceeding one million buttons per day, and a machinery plant that produced in-house all the needed tools, dies, and special machinery. While the Washington and Warren Street buildings fell victim to urban renewal, the 272 Sussex Street building remains standing, although divided into rental storage units.

Button Patents

W&H, which eventually claimed that it could produce over five thousand advertising specialty products, constantly made submissions to the US Patent and Trademark Office. Three patents are most relevant to their 1896 introduction of the pin-back button. A December 3, 1893, patent was filed by Amanda M. Lougee of Boston. W&H apparently purchased rights to this patent to protect their other claims, although the patent was for a cloth and metal clothing button. The second patent, filed December 6, 1895, established the reverse design of celluloid-covered pin-back buttons. Issued as a "jewelry" patent to George B. Adams (Adams was a Newark jewelry manufacturer who patented forty-nine different novelty articles), assignor to W&H, it specified "a shell with a marginal

rim to form a chamber and contain a continuous piece of wire with both a holding portion and a free end lying in the same plane." The third patent was filed March 23, 1896, and issued July 21, 1896, again to Adams. Although W&H was making pin-back buttons prior to July 21, 1896 (the earliest dated button we know of is for an Indiana State Medical Society annual meeting May 28–29, 1896, in Fort Wayne), we view this as the pin-back button's symbolic birthday. Six claims were made, each varying slightly, with Claim 1 reading:

> In a badge pin or button, in combination, with a shell having a marginal rim or bead, a covering bearing an inscription, design, emblem, or the like, over said shell and having its edges turned down over said marginal rim, a ring or collet in said shell placed over the edge of said covering to hold or secure the latter in position, and a bar or pin having one of its ends bent to form a holding portion adapted to be secured in said ring or collet, substantially as and for the purposes set forth.

In other words, W&H succeeded in producing a low-cost, wearable, and visually appealing mass-produced novelty. The pin-back button consisted of a clear sheet of celluloid over a printed circular paper with a metal backing. The reverse edges of the celluloid and paper were secured by a circular metal ring and worn by means of a brass wire pin inserted into the open reverse, with a pointed end for attachment to a fabric garment or hat.

The Button Department

W&H immediately became the world's largest button manufacturer, a title it held until its patents expired and the small printing press was developed. The immediate success of the button was astonishing.

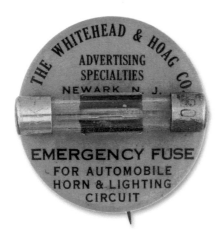

It debuted just a few months prior to the 1896 presidential nominating conventions and November's Election Day; W&H created over two thousand distinct button designs for McKinley and Bryan. Meanwhile, the company landed its first gigantic order from the American Tobacco Company to produce millions of buttons for insertion into product packages. It also made the first product advertising buttons for national firms and brands such as Heinz Baked Beans, King Arthur Flour, Wilbur's Cocoa, and Gold Medal Flour.

Button making, while quite mechanized, still required the insertion of the brass pin and W&H's promotional back paper into the button's open reverse by hand. The company solved the problem by offering payment for the work to children and families living around the factory. Thus, every day after school, children would come to the factory to pick up a box of buttons, pins, and back papers.

More and more advertisers and organizations felt compelled to have their own buttons. The subsequent presidential elections saw no diminishment of variety or quantity of buttons, and local candidates for every office found buttons the ideal medium to spread their messages. The high-quality color lithographic printing of this era distinguishes 1896 to 1912 as a distinct golden age of the button.

Branch Offices

The button's success naturally led to company expansion. By 1899, W&H had established sales offices in Baltimore, Boston, Buffalo, Chicago, Cincinnati, Detroit, New York, Philadelphia, and Pittsburgh. Outside the United States, offices were established in Buenos Aires, London, Melbourne, and Toronto. While all production took place in Newark, the branch offices were supplied with sample buttons to show potential customers. They also received from the Newark office a list of conventions being held in each city. The branch office salesmen, working on commission, would follow these leads and contact local businesses, churches, fraternal organizations, and political parties to solicit orders.

Post–World War I

In 1919, on the heels of World War I, a major reorganization took place at W&H. Benjamin Whitehead left the presidency and became chairman of the board. At the same time, W&H became a nonunion company.

Beginning in 1900, W&H back papers for buttons of all sizes carried the "Union Label" symbol of the Allied Printing Trades Council, Newark, New Jersey. While no longer a union plant after 1919, the company did not remove that symbol from their back papers until the end of 1929.

W&H began to experience increasing competition from other button making firms. Some paid to license their patents, but others created their own innovations in the button's construction to avoid paying W&H a licensing fee. Most important was the perfection of the process to make buttons solely from lithographed tin, prompted by the government's public relations effort to inspire patriotism and promote Liberty Loan bond sales during World War I. This type of button simply required printing repeating designs directly on a flat metal sheet. The design was then stamped out in the button shape, with a curved reverse edge capable of holding the spring pin. This eliminated the printed paper, the celluloid overlay, and the reverse collet, at a great savings of time, materials, and money. The result was a much narrower range of colors and a surface with paint that easily chipped and scratched. However, the process was ideal for many purposes, and while celluloid-covered buttons were clearly the higher-quality product, their use significantly decreased.

World War II

While World War II saw restrictions placed on the use of many metals, the button was largely exempted because of its usefulness in boosting home front patriotism, production, and morale. However, at W&H in Newark, normal button production ended, with few exceptions. Instead, using the material "Duroplastic," W&H launched into producing the millions upon millions of employee-identification buttons required by state and federal law. At the war's peak, W&H employed four hundred workers to produce these ID badges.

Sale to Bastian Brothers

Several factors led to W&H's decline by the late 1950s. The company had a long history of having a few very successful years followed by several years of operating at a loss. When Philip Hoag, Chester's son, died in 1953, no family member remained on the board or in a policymaking role. And (surprisingly, for a company that should have understood advertising) W&H refused to advertise any other place than on their own products.

In March 1959, W&H announced its upcoming sale. Bastian Brothers in Rochester, New York, was the firm's logical successor. Bastian was founded in 1895 and had been a longtime rival of W&H. As a union company, Bastian could not compete with W&H prices; like many other agents and jobbers, it would buy parts from and subcontract some of its work to W&H. The W&H factory closed in May 1959, and Bastian's president came to Newark to order its sale. Unusable machinery, dies, and tools were scrapped, and the W&H records of every item the company ever made were ordered destroyed. Most of the remaining branch salesmen became Bastian employees. Bastian continued to use W&H's name, eventually phasing it out by 1965.

Randolfe Wicker's Recollections of Underground Uplift Unlimited

I graduated from the University of Texas in 1960. I'd become involved in politics and found myself a $39.10-a-month, rent-controlled apartment in New York City's East Village, the mecca for everything new in New York. I'd wanted to be a journalist; however, after getting published in *The Nation* and producing unpaid programs for the subscriber-supported radio station WBAI-FM, I settled for the steady income supplied by editing pulp girlie magazines.

Civil rights campaign buttons had been popularized by Martin Luther King Jr.'s 1963 March on Washington. I'd discovered a shop custom printing buttons; five hundred was its minimum order, to cover the cost of typesetting and die making. On impulse, I risked twenty dollars publishing five hundred buttons reading "Replace Newbold Morris." Newbold Morris was the New York City Parks Commissioner who had ordered the city's Police Department to arrest folk singers performing around the fountain in Washington Square Park on weekends.

"Certainly, every merchant in Greenwich Village would want him gone," I reasoned. "People come to Greenwich Village on weekends for the free entertainment!"

I quickly discovered that neither the merchants nor the tourists around Washington Square Park even recognized the name Newbold Morris. Fortunately,

girlfriends and fans of the singers were delighted to help sell the buttons. Japanese tourists were their best customers: a slogan button in English was a genuine 25-cent souvenir of Americana. I gave the sellers half of whatever they took in. Even weeks later, I hadn't broken even. My first button was an absolute bust!

I've always considered myself a multifaceted activist. I was involved in civil rights, women's rights, and the anti–Vietnam War movements, as well as the most personal of issues—civil rights for homosexuals. Even getting stationery published for my Homosexual League of New York had been difficult. An order for matchbook covers had been declined. I decided to indulge myself and ordered one thousand buttons in lavender print on a white background reading "Equality for Homosexuals" (which cost only about five dollars more than five hundred). At that time, in the mid-1960s, nearly all gay people were in the closet. No one would dare wear that button. I didn't care—I just wanted to see it in print!

I'd been invited to a house party in Queens a few days after picking them up. My pockets full, I pinned one button onto my lapel and casually leaned against a wall.

"Where did you get that?" a fellow standing nearby blurted before I'd gotten the first sip of my drink.

"I print them," I replied. "Would you like to buy one?"

The price was 25¢ each—ten times what they had cost me. One by one, virtually every person at that party came over, introduced himself, and bought some buttons. That night I went home with more than thirty-nine dollars in my pocket.

My second button had shattered my expectations, and I was greedy for more. Every week, I'd publish another button: "Let's Legalize Pot," "I'm for Sexual Freedom," "Legalize Abortion," "Civilians Must Control Their Police," "Make Love, Not War." I commenced running ads in the *Village Voice*, and orders trickled in.

About a year after I'd started, I had recouped my money, and a whole new button culture was emerging. Buttons were conversation starters. Buttons indicated shared interests—whether that was smoking pot, anti-war politics, or astrology. You could communicate something profound, humorous, or just frivolous via buttons: "F*ck Censorship," "If you can read this button, you're standing too damn close!" "Mary Poppins is a Junkie."

In 1966, Mike Quill, who'd organized New York City subway workers, called a strike and brought urban life to a screeching halt. Mark Sloan, a comedy club doorman who dabbled in selling buttons from a four-by-six-foot souvenir shop on MacDougal Street, began selling large, yellow buttons saying "TO HELL WITH QUILL" in heavy, black letters. I used to wholesale some of my buttons to Mark Sloan. When I saw him flash several hundred-dollar bills one evening over coffee, I decided it was time to open a store of my own.

I opened my small shop at 28 St. Marks Place, on what would become the central thoroughfare for East Coast hippiedom. I'd covered the opening of a small art gallery that was closing, and I snapped up the lease for $100 a month. I set up my shop using little metal cabinets set on wooden chairs. The first weekend, I took in $289. I'd never seen so many one- and five-dollar bills. I put them in a huge pile and took Polaroid pictures to show the family.

My shop became New York City's first button-poster-psychedelic shop on the East Coast. I let anybody put any leaflets or publications on a free literature table. For a while, I called my business Free Speech Inc. Later, it became Underground Uplift Unlimited. You could get a Day-Glo poster of your favorite rock band or a "William F. Buckley for Mayor" poster. After I'd sold thousands of "Dump Johnon" buttons, the *New York Times* started calling the anti–Vietnam War movement the "Dump Johnson" movement.

Business boomed. I grossed two hundred thousand dollars in my first year and netted forty thousand. I'd wisely developed a nationwide market for the buttons that were at the core of my business. Students put themselves through school at universities as far away as Berkeley, California, and Colorado by purchasing my buttons for seventy-five dollars per thousand and then reselling them for twenty-five or fifty cents each.

I closed my shop in 1971. Underground Uplift Unlimited would live on as Uplift Incorporated—my corporate name—until I closed my last business, an art deco lighting shop in the West Village, in 2003. A lot of tensions are growing in the world today; I've seen numerous small entrepreneurs selling buttons at the Women's Marches and at climate change events. An African American man in his seventies sells portrait buttons of famous African American and Native American writers and activists. If I weren't eighty-one years old, I'd be tempted to dive back in. It's great to be in the mix of things, helping to make the world a little better of a place.

Randolfe (Randy) Wicker
Hoboken, New Jersey, 2019

About the Authors

Christen Carter has been a fan of buttons since she was twelve, when they were one of the few items cheap enough for her to buy with her own money. She loves how buttons are distilled graphic representations of thoughts that are meant to be shared. Christen founded the Chicago-based Busy Beaver Button Company in 1995 and has produced more than fifty million buttons for bands, artists, political campaigns, and others. In 2010, she started the Button Museum, a nonprofit institution with an educational mission to explore US history through pin-back buttons.

Here are a few of Christen's most personally important buttons, with her recollections:

1. While living in London in 1995 on a work program through my college, I met Mark Pawson, a button maker who had been a customer of the legendary punk button company Better Badges (see page 46). Mark started making buttons out of his London apartment in 1984 for his own art and for other artists. We met at a lecture given by Cynthia Plaster Caster and Jamie Reid (fittingly, as Reid was the designer of badges for the Sex Pistols and others). A few days later, Mark showed me how to make buttons, and upon my return to the States, I started Busy Beaver Button Company. Busy Beaver is known for bringing the 1-inch button back into use during the DIY (do it yourself) / punk scene of the 1990s.

2. When I was twelve, my family went to London for vacation. It was a big deal, and I had saved a little babysitting money to get souvenirs and gifts. I really loved Woodstock, maybe even a little more than Snoopy, so I was thrilled to find this button—a bright holographic button with Snoopy unicycling and juggling! It made me part of an unofficial club of *Peanuts* enthusiasts. I really like how the makers of this button took the extra effort to add the smallest dot of yellow for Woodstock. They could have used the same yellow as the background but went the extra distance to give him an extra spot of his own color.

3. This is the first punk button I ever bought. One of my brothers was (and still very much is) a guitar fanatic, so we'd go to the House of Guitars in Rochester, New York. The basement was full of records and organized in all sorts of confusing ways, so it was easy to spend a lot of time there. After looking through records, I would examine the rotating kiosk of buttons at the cash register, which featured various types of buttons: heavy metal, pop, punk rock, and funny sayings. I bought this one and wore it so proudly, hoping I'd find people who liked the same music I did and maybe wanting a few coolness points to rub off of X, onto me.

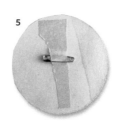

4. Ted is a great gift giver—especially when it comes to buttons. I had been looking for this one and was so pleased when one day it showed up. It's a simple two-color button but very sophisticated! As a manufacturer, I am interested in innovative uses of materials and components. The celluloid was printed on its back side with brown and white, allowing the die-cut shape of a hat to expose the actual felt that Lanpher's hats were made of. The felt can be felt, making this button not only a visual item but also a tactile one.

5. In high school I ran for student council president. I didn't have a button maker, so I instead got my hands on cardboard, markers, scissors, masking tape, and safety pins and made these mock buttons. We won by a landslide. What strikes me now is that from a young age, I've believed that buttons are powerful idea sharers and community builders.

6. When I give tours at the Button Museum, people sometimes ask me what my favorite button is. There are forty thousand to choose from, so it's difficult. I say as much and then pull out one of the above buttons to discuss; then I say, "But *this* is the ultimate button!" A laugh or groan usually follows—this button does its job and does it well.

More at buttonmuseum.org

Ted Hake has been a collector since the age of eight and a button dealer since the age of eighteen. In 1967, he founded Hake's Auctions, America's first auction house to specialize in popular-culture artifacts. He has written seventeen collectors' guides that span presidential campaign items, vintage Disneyana, and comic character toys. For decades, Ted helped children's book author and artist Maurice Sendak build his 1930s-era Mickey Mouse collection. (Sendak's book *In the Night Kitchen* includes a cityscape building labeled Hake Coffee as a thank-you to Ted for providing product advertising buttons that Sendak used in creating his illustrations.) Ted has received the American Political Items Collectors Lifetime Achievement Award and is a member of the Theodore Roosevelt Association Advisory Board.

These are some of Ted's favorites:

1. Patented in 1861, Cahoon's Seed Sower claimed to allow the user to distribute seeds throughout four to eight acres in an hour, walking at a normal pace. The device was strapped to the chest and operated by a hand crank. This superbly designed button depicts a gentleman farmer in his field, with tiny broken lines representing flying seeds spiraling in all directions. Based on the button's inscription, "50 Years of Success," this Bastian Brothers–designed button was issued for the device's fiftieth anniversary in 1911.

2. In 2016, the button was repurposed by Hake's Auctions' Americana specialist, Scott Mussell, as a surprise for me; it was produced, of course, by Christen Carter and the Busy Beaver Button Company. Scott and I cochaired the American Political Items Collectors 2016 national convention. At the Saturday night dinner, when I received APIC's Lifetime Achievement Award, some three hundred APIC members received a 1½-inch replica of my favorite button—to my immense surprise, picturing me.

3. I became aware of buttons at age five in 1948. My mother's antique-dealer friend gave me a small, gray box holding about twenty World War I Liberty Loan promotion and War Chest contributor buttons. The box remained in my secret drawer until I rediscovered buttons in 1960.

4. In the fall of 1966, I was a grad student at NYU's film school. The journey by subway from my part-time job at the Museum of Modern Art's film vault in Long Island City took me through the East Village on my way to classes. At 28 St. Marks Place, I discovered Randolfe Wicker's recently opened store, Underground Uplift Unlimited (see APPENDIX B). I traded a quarter for my first 1960s slogan button: Nirvana Needed.

5. Maurice Sendak gave me this unique hand-drawn button around 1985, while I was visiting his Connecticut home to show him early-1930s Mickey Mouse collectibles, one of his diverse collecting passions. He told me that in 1983 he had attended a conference where his hosts offered to make a button for his personal use during the event. He drew the art on the spot, and thanks to the Badge-A-Minit amateur button-making machine popular in that decade, presto—a pretty special button!

6. My first Hake's Americana & Collectibles advertising button was ordered from cartoonist and underground comix publisher Denis Kitchen. In 1975, he tasked his Cartoon Factory stalwart artist Peter Poplaski (later known for his Superman comic book covers and work on Spider-Man) with the project.

7. In 2014, when I launched my personal website, Busy Beaver Button Company's Christen Carter suggested and Abbey Hambright designed this modern version of me wearing my 1975 button.

More at tedhake.com

Acknowledgments

The authors' greatest debt of gratitude is extended to all the collectors since 1896 who preserved pinback buttons for posterity. Foremost among these collectors were Joseph L. Stone of Toledo, Ohio, and Marshall N. Levin of New York City.

Stone began his collection in 1921 with a single button plucked, on a whim, from a street gutter while he was on an errand to buy a loaf of bread for his mother. By the time of Joe's death in 1975, the ever-expanding collection well exceeded fifty thousand buttons pinned to thick sheets of black felt suspended from the perimeter of the ceiling of his "button room." Since that time, largely via Hake's Auctions, Stone's buttons, many of which are the sole example known to this day, have joined thousands of collections across the United States.

Levin left an ad agency job in the early 1960s to freelance as a medical journal writer. Somehow, at the same time, he acquired a passion for button collecting, which for the next four decades was a passion realized. He was the first (and eminently most successful) collector to visit the dozen or so New York City button making companies in quest of old stock, samples of current button runs, and, most important, a lasting relationship that would deliver the button goods to be made in future weeks, months, and years. Levin's collecting efforts extended beyond the city's button makers to every possible trade show, political convention, and, beginning around 1965, the many political and social issue demonstrations that became a hallmark of the decade. If an acquired button was not dated on the front, Levin would notate a "master button" for his collection, in ink on the metal reverse, with the month/year acquired and other crucial information such as the issuer's name and sometimes even the quantity produced. By the time of Levin's death in 1999, his spacious prewar Greenwich Village apartment was home to hundreds of thousands of buttons—counting the duplicates he used for trading (he never sold, only traded)—most of them a single example documenting American life and its detail from the most macro perspective down to the most micro.

Almost all modern-day, collector-assembled, pinback button collections—including our own—have benefited from those originally established and nurtured by Stone and Levin. For this book, we supplemented our own collections by reaching out to friends and longtime collectors. For trusting us with your treasures and for sharing them with a wider circle of friends, we are deeply grateful to Lon Ellis, Jonell Hake, Scott Mussell, Phil Shimkin, Leka Mladenovic, and Alex Winter of Hake's Auctions.

For historical information on the Whitehead & Hoag Co., we appreciate the research of Gary Patterson and the personal experiences shared by Chester R. Hoag's granddaughter Verdenal (Verdi) Hoag Johnson. Staff and resources at the Newark Museum, the Newark Public Library, and the Jefferson R. Burdick collection at the Metropolitan Museum of Art were also most helpful.

We are also grateful for the advice and assistance of Joel Carter, Bob Cereghino, Milton Glaser, David Holcomb, Ken and Cathy Hosner, Christy Karpinski, Hannah Mann, Joanna Metger, John O'Brien, John Pfeifer, Ward Reilly, Brett Sova, Divya Srinivasan, Randolfe Wicker, and David Yount.

And a deeply felt thank you to our photographers, with us every step of a one-year project that took five, Terence and Robin Kean of Kean Design Studio. Christy Karpinski aided with supplemental photography.

We also much appreciate the guidance of Andrea Morrison, our agent at Writer's House, and our outstanding team at Princeton Architectural Press of Sara McKay, Sara Stemen, and Ben English.

Christen would also like to thank her (very large) family.

Our thanks to one and all who helped us share our love for buttons.

Christen Carter & Ted Hake
April 2020

THIS BUTTON
SUPERCEDES
ALL PREVIOUS
BUTTONS

1970

Published by
Princeton Architectural Press
202 Warren Street
Hudson, New York 12534
www.papress.com

Editor: Sara Stemen
Designer: Benjamin English

Library of Congress Cataloging-in-Publication Data
NAMES: Carter, Christen, author. | Hake, Theodore L., author.
TITLE: Button power / Christen Carter and Ted Hake.
DESCRIPTION: New York : Princeton Architectural Press, [2020] |
   Summary: "A collection of more than 2,000 colorful and artistic
   pin-back buttons, forming a people's history of American culture
   and politics that focuses on a range of subjects: advertising,
   arts and entertainment, historical events, movements and
   causes, humor, nature, celebrated personalities and organizations,
   geographical features, sports, transportation, wars and anti-
   war movements" —Provided by publisher.
IDENTIFIERS: LCCN 2019058508 | ISBN 9781616898700 (hardcover)
SUBJECTS: LCSH: Pin-back buttons—United States—Collectors and
   collecting—Catalogs. | United States—History—1865–
CLASSIFICATION: LCC NK3670 .C35 2020 | DDC 737/.24075—dc23
LC RECORD AVAILABLE AT: https://lccn.loc.gov/2019058508

All button dates are approximate year of issue.
Buttons have been enlarged (and in rare cases reduced)
when they appear alongside a caption or in a thematic
grid. All others are shown at actual size.

Image Credits
36: An emotional Beatles fan at the Indiana State Fair in Indianapolis, September 4, 1964. Associated Press/Bob Daugherty
62: A delegate at the Democratic National Convention,
   Miami Beach, Florida, 1972. Copyright © Diana Mara Henry/
   www.dianamarahenry.com
68: Little Bird, a member of the Arapaho tribe, wearing a William
   McKinley button at the 1898 Trans-Mississippi and International
   Exposition in Omaha, Nebraska. Frank A. Rhinehart, courtesy
   Boston Public Library
72: Janine Andrews sporting buttons from the Badge Shop
   in Covent Garden, London, January 1981. Trinity Mirror/
   Mirrorpix/Alamy Stock Photo
90: Girls wearing Obama 2012 inauguration buttons, Washington,
   DC, January 21, 2013. B Christopher/Alamy Stock Photo
98: Student on Old Clothes Day at Hempstead High School, May 27,
   1958. Gordon Parks/Getty Images
120: Black Panther Party members outside the New York City Crim-
   inal Courts Building, April 11, 1969. David Fenton/Getty Images
136: Cesar Chavez wearing a button protesting Chiquita, April 20,
   1979. Marion S. Trikosko, courtesy Library of Congress
144: Martin Luther King Jr. on Capital Hill delivering his "I Have
   a Dream" speech, wearing a button designed for the event,
   August 28, 1963. Rolls Press/Popperfoto via Getty Images